THE
AUDACITY
OF
FRIENDSHIP

THE
AUDACITY
OF
FRIENDSHIP

Finding Community
IN THE
Age of Isolation

GREG BOOKS

ILLUMIFY
MEDIA.COM

The Audacity of Friendship
Copyright © 2024 by Gregory Books, PhD

Published by
Illumify Media Global
www.IllumifyMedia.com
"Let's bring your book to life!"

Paperback ISBN: 978-1-959099-80-2

Cover design by Debbie Lewis
Author photo by Art Eichmann
Printed in the United States of America

Contents

Introduction

We live in an age of extreme technology, and the paradox of technology is that the more we have, the less connection we feel to one another. One way we can see this is in the overuse of the word "community." Can you think of a news article, interview, blog posting, or event that doesn't overuse the word? If every winner of a hot dog eating contest tells us that their goal is to inspire and empower others, and give something back to the community, what does that tell us about how they see the world around them? Depressed, powerless, impoverished, and disconnected. If what they seek is a safe space, doesn't that tell us that their view of the world is as a place of danger? This is because our public speech isn't about what we have; it's about what we don't have. The overuse of the term "community" is a clear indication that we don't experience community. The word "community" is a metaphor for an unexpressed desire for connection.

Critics of modern life often point to the internet, or the iPhone, or some other personal device which connects us to the hive mind as the culprit in our loss of community. But others recognize that the long-term influence of a much earlier technology has created the habits of thought and expression that have led to our current isolation. The invention is writing: the technology of converting sound to object on a flat page.

We usually don't think of literacy as a technology. But the act of converting sounds that occur in time, in the presence of others, into black marks on a flat page, is a technology. Like all inventions, first users adapt themselves to using it, and succeeding generations of users simply can't imagine life any other way. We often create modifying terms for the new technology to differentiate it from the old (electric guitar, digital gauges), and when the new technology becomes standard, we invent terms to describe the old (acoustic guitar; steam gauges). We may continue using terminology of the pre-tech era (do you dial your phone?). As we age, we find ourselves telling our kids about how we grew up without it. The current pace of technological growth is so fast that my two children, born twelve years apart, had extremely different experiences. The oldest, born in 1990, grew up with cassette tapes and the first iPod. The youngest, born in 2002, never saw an iPod outside of the junk drawer, and the idea of not having twenty-four-hour-per-day access to his favorite song through a device on his wrist is unthinkable. Even the idea of watching a television program when it comes on (what? Make an appointment to watch a show?) seems strange to him.

But while our experience of music has changed through streaming, there's still a high value placed on old recording equipment. Some of us prefer to hear music in the way it was meant to be heard...on vinyl! Many can even discern the difference between digital and analog recording, and the experience that each produces. Some even have continued to use analog recording devices because of the difference.

I've written this book because I believe that there are elements of value to be found in ancient ways of thinking about community. Oral cultures think of the self and the community in very different ways than do modern literate cultures. And in what follows, I suggest that one important pathway to regain community is not to plunge forward into increasing technological disconnection, but by recovering our understanding of community from an oral stance. That means going back and listening to Scripture through analog sound.

You might think this is absurd, since all the world is digital. And here is where I disagree with many others. We are born as oral beings, and throughout time, most cultures have been and remain oral. Of the 10,000 estimated languages spoken in the world today, only about 300 have a written literature. In short, we are born oral, and a small fraction of us learn to think through literacy. Throughout history, only a handful of us become truly literate. And the literacy that we attain is hard to develop, unstable, and takes an enormous amount of energy to maintain. Further, our thought leaders are far more literate than most people in the trenches ever become. For instance, it's generally accepted that fewer than 1 in 100 people could read and write in Paul's day. Ninety-nine of his hearers only heard his letters as they were read in public. Their understanding of community was very different than how we think of it today. In today's common usage, community means everyone reading this internet posting, or anyone who is remotely interested in our issue, or lives within our geographical area, or whose ancestors came from the same country. That's almost the opposite of oral cultures, who experience community as the outcome of shared experiences, values, beliefs, rituals, and proximity. In the modern, literate world, we insist that the only experience we share is the complete inability to understand any experience, belief, or even truth outside of our own individual feelings.

I write primarily to modern-day believers, because worship groups are the only element in American life that recognize, prioritize, and celebrate shared beliefs. What other institution can you name that meets every week to worship? Even sports events have divided worship, but faith communities meet to worship the same deity. Where else will you find people who regularly teach and assent to the idea that your concerns are greater than mine, your welfare more pressing, and your edification more important than my own? Where else do people believe and teach that there is no greater love than to give up our own life for another? Where else do we even pretend to have a shared sense of purpose, destiny, and calling? Certainly not in American politics, or cultural activism! In fact, faith teaches us that our identity is outside of politics and activism.

Some may protest that believing and teaching concepts doesn't mean that we live up to them. That may or may not be true, but it doesn't take away from the fact that we still talk about community in ways that are diametrically opposed to radical individualism and isolation. Even if we fail, we fail together!

Of more concern is that those of us who lead faith communities are double minded when it comes to teaching about relationships. All Christian teaching is about relationships: with our Creator, ourselves, our spouses, our families, and our neighbors. Yet most of our teaching materials about relationships are based on mid-twentieth century psychology, which was largely hostile to faith. As oral beings, we may feel that something is slightly off, and if we could put words to it, we might say that what our hearts tell us about relationships doesn't line up with the teaching. Part of what follows is to identify how listeners of the first century discussed relationships, instead of projecting modern sensibilities into the past.

For example, Jesus told us "I have called you friends." The popular usage of "friend" has changed multiple times even in the last two decades. Current usage ranges from wanting to see more photos of your cat to a threat. Formal theories of "friendship" are based on three types of models: manipulation and compliance gaining, game theory, or economic exchange. None of these theories existed before 1950. Wouldn't it make sense to read what people in the first century thought about friendship before we tell ourselves that Jesus wants be our friend? Especially since the threat that moved Pilate to give up an innocent man to execution was the rumor that he was not a friend to Ceasar?

So how could we go about recovering an oral sense of community? That's a tall order, especially through writing. But here's where we start: with three grand stories or narratives.

The first story of this book explores some of the differences between orality and literacy. We try to recover some of the elements of an oral experience. To do this, we listen to how oral cultures think about the self, how they think about time, and how they would think about the notion of success. This becomes a context for understanding how technologies (like writing) redefine those elements of experience.

The second story explores how modern day theories of the self and relationships originated and became almost universal. How did we come to think about all relationships as if they were poker games, including our relationship to God?

The third story focuses on friendship, and how an oral understanding of that relationship still exists in spite of the formal models that we think we believe. What if we were to take Jesus' invitation to friendship and live it as a model of the way we can relate to others? Not in the modern sense of a card game, a penny stock, or a guilt trip, but in the ancient, oral sense of selfless commitment?

To begin to get a sense of how different it may have been, consider: if you read Isaiah, you'll find many instances where the prophet was told to speak a message, but only a few where he was told to write something. In those few instances, they were proclamations of judgment, death, and destruction. Life, hope, comfort, and promise were spoken; judgment and death were written. This pattern holds true throughout the Old Testament: promise and life are proclaimed by speaking, death and destruction through writing. In the New Testament era, every time a written decree went out from Rome, lives were disrupted, and people died. Even the events of Jesus' birth were because of a decree (written) of taxation that disrupted the life of everyone who wasn't at their ancestral home. This pattern holds until the invention of inexpensive printing fifteen centuries later. Writing almost always signifies death in some way. Is it any wonder that Paul says writing kills, but speaking brings life? Or that when the written law comes in, death enters?

Of course, there's a major paradox here. I'm writing about an oral experience. That's like singing about how something smells. Is it even possible? One way to do it is by writing as if I were telling stories rather than delivering a lecture. The latter is about moving information from my brain to yours in an attempt to get you to think like me. The lecture format developed not to aid retention, but to facilitate testing. A story is more about opening up speculation, application, and reflection. Good storytellers don't tell you how the story ends before they start. They may give you a reason for telling the story, but they don't tell you what the story means. That's because good stories always have more meanings than can be articulated, and why good stories end up leaving more questions than they do answers. So I've written in what another writer (thanks, Burt Levy) calls "first-person barstool." As I write, I'm imagining that you and I are sitting in my eastern office (Two Brothers Restaurant) with two empty plates and a fresh refill of coffee in front of us. Like all good stories, this one may wander off the path and smell flowers along the way. Or speculate about just how sharp the wolf's teeth may be. Or just how sweet the gingerbread shingles are.

1
Technologies of Literacy

I've come up with a set of rules that describes our reactions to technologies:

1. Anything that is in the world when you're born is normal and ordinary and is just a natural part of the way the world works.
2. Anything that's invented between when you're fifteen and thirty-five is new and exciting and revolutionary and you can probably get a career in it.
3. Anything invented after you're thirty-five is against the natural order of things.

Douglas Adams, *The Salmon of Doubt*

Around the fourth century BCE, a revolutionary invention happened—one that forever changed our understanding of ourselves, our world, and our relationship to God. No one knows who actually is responsible for this invention, but the long-range effects that it introduced are truly astounding. Over the next several centuries, its effects slowly changed the way that people thought about everything: from God, to existence, to the very nature of thought itself. In fact, prior to this invention, we were not capable of asking what it even was to think. Analytic thought (the slicing of truth into small segments in order to test the consistency of the parts against the whole), which is very familiar to us, could not exist prior to this invention.

For those in the Christian tradition, the technology of writing first worked its influence in Greece, and from there spread to Rome in the years around the first century. While Rome didn't adopt the invention until the fourth century, it was influenced by its borrowing from Greek culture. Other nations and cultures were more resistant to this invention, with the result that they retained much of the older way of living until several centuries later. Some, like Israel, were dispersed through military conquest before they could be shaped by this invention.

Today, we have very little understanding of life before the change, but to someone in the midst of a wholesale cultural shift, life was tumultuous. The invention: the alphabet. The result: writing slowly replaced talk as the locus of knowledge and the primary way of experiencing the world. Prior to the thorough dispersion of the new technology of writing, all cultural knowledge was contained in oral stories, songs, poems, and other verbal forms. Long poems like *The Iliad* and *The Odyssey* were sung as entertainment, but they also instructed the hearers in how to live virtuous lives in their communities. To hear the story of Priam's actions was to hear the marks of bravery and competence in early Greek society. Much like our fairytale stories of today, oral stories were instruction and entertainment wrapped up in one oral performance. But what happens when knowledge is thought to be true because it is written down, and instruction becomes a formal exercise and the responsibility of an elite who can read and write?

Scholars have traced the wrenching effects on a culture when literacy—the use of reading and writing to order and transmit knowledge—overtakes and replaces orality. Yet even in civilizations where literacy is the primary technology, vestigial forms of orality remain.

This shift from orality to literacy has tremendous implications for readers of the Bible. The historical fact is that the Bible existed in oral form long before it was written. The Old Testament is the written record of several thousand years of retelling the stories of Israel. While the New Testament was written, it was written to and by people who still retained much of their oral cast of mind. Thus, it was spoken first and then written.

In short, the Bible was not regarded as a *written* document until well into the second century CE, and even then, it was treated as the written record of oral encounters. But the differences between the spoken word, for oral and literate cultures, are as great as the differences between night and day, or between computer literacy and computer illiteracy.

This book explores some of the differences that might occur, and raises the continual question, "What might this have sounded like to someone who thought not like us, but who thought of word and power, language and reality, as an oral thinker?" This question differs from traditional textual studies, which might ask the question, "What did Paul actually *say*?" It differs from philosophical and theological study, which would ask, "What did Paul *mean*?" It will be a rhetorical study, in that we will always ask the question, "What would Paul's audience have heard against the backdrop of Greek thought?"

While we will never be able to truly recover an oral sense of the Bible, and what it was like in its original performative context, we can attempt to attenuate the resonance of a sound heard millennia ago. We can capture a slight resonance of the sound of songs sung long ago.

Oral vs. Literate Cultures

Now, let's talk about some of the differences between oral and literate cultures. One difference is that literate readers believe that speaking and writing are the same. When we see a reference to speaking in Scripture, we substitute writing and reading as if they were the same as speaking and hearing. We shift from a *presentation* to a *representation*. To the oral mind, squiggles on the page *represent* something that was spoken, but the hearers wouldn't regard the marks as the act of speaking. The marks aren't the sound of a voice; they represent the sound of a voice reduced to a visual depiction.

For example, Romans 10:17 tells us that faith comes by hearing, and hearing by the Word of God. Most of the time, we read the verse silently, and we substitute *reading* for *hearing*. It becomes "faith comes by reading, and reading the written Word of God in isolation." And no wonder; we're encouraged to read our Bibles daily, to memorize the verses, and to read as much as we can to bolster our faith. To be sure, reading the Bible can be encouraging, and what we learn from reading can sustain and build our faith. But reading is not the same as hearing. We see the same switch happening when people start a written paragraph with the phrase "that being said" when nothing has been said. *Saying* and *writing* (or *typing*) are regarded as the same, but there are a number of differences.

First, notice that I've given you the Scripture reference at the top of the section, which is a common way to introduce a Bible passage. But think about what that does; it offers proof that I'm not misusing a verse, since you can look it up yourself and read it to check me. If I don't give the Scripture reference, it could undermine your confidence in what I'm writing.

In other words (see how I've used *words* to refer to writing here?), giving the Scripture reference says more about me than it does about you. It tells you that you can trust me. It is self-referential, and it functions to bolster my credibility. Those reference numbers were added by translators as an easy index to find verses, but my repeating them just tells you that I'm knowledgeable. Even though it's a subtle change, adding the Scripture reference shifts the question of authority to *me* in addition to the Word. Nowhere does Paul, Jesus, or any of the apostolic composers give chapter and verse for what they quote in their sermons and letters.

Second, Paul didn't write this. He spoke it. Someone else captured it and put it into writing, as all writing was composed in the first century. And it wasn't meant to be read silently, but to be read aloud so that it could have meaning. It's an important point, but squiggles on a flat page have no meaning to an oral mind. They must be translated into sound for any benefit to occur.

Because of this, all learning in an oral culture must happen in community, never alone. There must be a speaker as well as a hearer. Even in the first century, those who could read still depended on oral discussion and instruction to gain meaning from the page. We can hear this in the account of the Ethiopian court official in the book of Acts. Philip hears him reading the book of Isaiah aloud, and he asks the official if he understands what he reads (aloud). The official asks, "How can I unless someone is there to speak the meaning?" This is orality speaking; even the few who could read treated writing as visual prompts to recover an act of speaking rather than as an analog of speech.

Imagine that you received your next phone operating system upgrade as a set of written code. Unless you could translate that code into imaginary functions, it would be meaningless. It would simply be marks on a page. In the same way, oral hearers of the first century didn't go into isolation to read the Word and grow in faith; they gathered to hear it proclaimed and explained. Scripture is full of messengers who speak to Creation, whether angels (messengers), apostles (those who are sent), or even donkeys. All speak messages that correct, instruct, convict, and encourage.

In the same way, they didn't pray silently in private only; they lifted up their voices and prayed communally. We see this in Jesus, who went to the place of prayer as was His custom, and took along some of His closest friends. Think of the implications of Jesus saying that wherever two or three were gathered in His name, He would be present. What they would hear would be that whenever they got together to pray or discuss what He has said to them, He would already be in their midst! Notice that hearing this through an oral mind doesn't change the meaning, but it broadens the application. It enriches our understanding, opening up new possibilities rather than nailing down all possible meanings to one.

This is because a *presentational* view of language sees speaking as creating rather than reporting. Here's a good example. We're all familiar with what some of the names meant in the Old Testament. We know that people's names were changed after they had an encounter with the Holy One. We know that Jacob's name was changed from "supplanter" to "Israel" because he'd wrestled with God and found favor. As literate thinkers, we choose names for our children because they sound good, are popular, or honor others.

The oral mind chooses names *because* they have meanings, and speaking the name brings something into being. To name your son "courage" was to create something, and to set a course for him to grow up to act courageously. To name your daughter Prudence (one of the most popular female names in eighteenth-century America) was to inculcate that virtue as the one for which she would be known.

Imagine calling your son Ariel ("lion of God"). Every time you spoke his name, you were instilling in him the qualities of a lion. "Come in for lunch, Lion of God. Your SpaghettiOs are ready!" or "Hey, Lion of God, pick up your LEGOs. I don't want to step on them in the middle of the night!" Every time you spoke his name, you were unleashing a force that would shape and guide who he was becoming in the world. Naming was critical in who you brought up the child to be in their community.

Imagine having two sons, and calling one Ahitub ("my brother is goodness") and the other Ichabod ("the glory has departed"). These were the names of the two sons of Phineas, whose sin caused the Israelites to be defeated in battle, and the Ark of the Covenant to be captured by the Philistines. Every time you called the name Ichabod, you'd be proclaiming the loss of God's glory and the defeat and subjugation of your people because of human folly. Of course this would have power-ful implications for this child's self-image, but more importantly, these names would serve as constant reminders of God's blessing and judg-ment in their midst.

Not only did names have meaning, and were chosen because they were creative, but the names often drove the story in powerful ways. When Abraham and Sarah name their son Isaac, it's a powerful moment, and every time the story is told, the hearer is reminded that the "con-tentious one" (Sarai) becomes a "princess" (Sarah) when "God's laughter" (Isaac) enters her life!

Literacy has turned our attention away from the fact that names have declarative power and shape the story; now names are only an interesting part of the story. We don't even think of names until we're reminded of them. We don't live in the echo of the transformation every time a name is changed. Unlike Ruth ("pleasant"), who declares, "Call me Mara ["bitter"], for the Almighty hath dealt very bitterly with me" (Ruth 1:20 KJV), we don't hear a name as a declaration of identity because of what God has done in a person's life.

The adoption of literacy thins out the power of the tongue, and turns our attention away from the question, "What do words do?" to "What do words mean?" It's a shift from *declaring* to *defining*, from *creating* to *critiquing*, and from *making* to *measuring*. In our modern world, we think of words as representing an idea or expressing an opinion. We talk about "speaking out" as if we (the self) are trapped inside our bodies, unseen and opaque to others around us. Our words become a way of trying to bridge between the inner and outer person—what others see as opposed to who we think we are. This is dualism, the belief that we are spirits trapped inside fleshly containers.

But what of it? Why is the distinction between an oral reception of Scripture and a written experience important? Why should we care, and, more importantly, why should we consider the differences?

Three Challenges

This book raises three challenges to our literate way of understanding Scripture, and to how we use Scripture to ground our communities. The difference between orality and literacy is more than just icing on the cake, or details of a culture that are only known to us through writing. These challenges constitute true paradigm changes.

1. **Modern notions of success versus the oral concept of faithfulness.** The concept of success depends on literacy. I will raise the question, "Is our modern concept of success to be found in Scripture?" I don't mean "How does our modern standard of success compare to a first-century standard of success?" Success depends on the comparison of ourselves to others, or comparison of ourselves to ourselves. Instead, the standard found in oral cultures is faithfulness, which depends on whether we've done what we are commanded to do. Many of the parables speak of people who we would judge as failures, but whom Jesus commended for being faithful.

2. **Modern notions of time, which arise from literacy.** Past, present, and future are determined in our minds by the linearity of writing. To us, time flows from a beginning point to an end point in the future—from left to right on a flat surface. Time is sharply divided into small boxes that we can see on our digital calendars, starting on the upper left, moving across to the right, and stacked one week on top of another. Hours of the day are shown to us in numbers or on a dial. But is this how ancient and modern oral cultures think of time? When "eternity steps into time" (to borrow from Michael Card), is it the same? We think of the past behind us, the future ahead of us, and the present as a fiction, and we move toward a goal with visible results. Oral cultures think of time as a circle, with

the future behind, the past in front, and the present as the past in the repeated story or festival. Guidance comes through a voice, not sight. We try to overcome our past by putting it behind us, while oral cultures embrace their past by keeping it in front of them.

3. **Modern notions of the self and relationships to others**. Are the models of relationships that ground what we teach our churches to be found in Scripture, or are they a late-twentieth-century sensibility projected into the past? If a first-century oral understanding of self and our relationship to others is different, how would it change the way we teach about our relationship to God, to each other in families, to our congregations as communities, and to the communities that we have been placed into and called to affect?

Of course, the answer is always, "Yes, modern literate thinking is very different," or I wouldn't be writing the book. But the story is an important one, and the challenge to our paradigm is helpful. What we'll find along the way is that we are intuitively oral, by creation and by nature. Literacy is a technology that produces patterns of thought, but those patterns aren't our natural state.

All children are oral, which is why they so often frustrate us parents who would just like them to act like adults! It takes years of education to produce a literate thinker, and the literacy that is produced is fragile and unstable. In short, we are oral beings with a veneer of literacy. This is why we often are split between what our hearts tell us and what our minds tell us. Our hearts are oral, and our minds struggle to be literate. It's also why we respond so quickly to stories, and why songs engage our emotions so much more than sights.

Along the way, we'll have to spend some time understanding how we think about time, the self and relationships, and faithfulness, and how we came to think this way. We'll have to spend some time looking at the history of theories about these things, and that can get a little dry.

But put on your swimsuit, plug your nose, gird your loins, put up your tray table, and jump in. I promise the effort will be worth it. At the conclusion, we'll think about how an oral understanding of what we hear in Scripture can enrich our teaching, bless our congregations, and give greater honor to God. I'd also like to assure you that none of what you learn will change the Gospel. It's still the good news!

2
Orality and Literacy

Imagine that you were born into a culture with no ability to write. Everything that needed to be learned had to be taught verbally. You couldn't write anything down, so there was no way to take notes to refer back to at another time. You couldn't store what you had learned in some physical location to later retrieve it, nor could you point someone who wanted to learn the same things to a book or a newspaper. You knew only what you could remember, and could remember only what you had heard. How would your thinking differ?

First, your hearing would need to be much more acute. You would have to be aware of the subtle differences between sounds as they are heard, since you couldn't rely on writing to clarify questions. Individual differences between words would be much more important, perhaps to the extent of marking the difference between life and death. So, if someone remarked, "No man is an island," it might prompt a moment of philosophical reflection, but if you were to hear the statement as "no mayonnaise in Ireland," you'd wonder what the Irish put on sandwiches. As you might guess, regional differences in pronunciation, no matter how slight, would be of great consequence in marking you as an outsider to the community.

Your attention span would need to be much greater than it is today, and you would probably need to develop a much greater memory in order to keep track of what you knew. Since what you could remember would be the total of what you knew, you'd probably learn ways of rehearsing what you knew to keep it fresh and alive. As an individual, you'd learn ways of putting your knowledge to song or rhyme as a way of remembering and passing it along. Your community would develop a storyteller role that would be much different from the storyteller roles we have today.

For one thing, storytellers would be far more important than bricklayers, since bricklayers can be trained in a matter of months. But when a storyteller dies, there must be another in his or her place, fully trained and having earned the respect of the community. Without the stories that constitute the community, the community ceases to exist.

Not only would your attention span be greater and your memory more fully developed, but the kinds of verbal patterns you used would change as well. You'd probably find yourself looping back in conversation to assist the memory of the hearer, and you might find yourself using much more descriptive language. You'd have more colorful expressions, figures of speech, and word devices to ensure that your words stood out more clearly. All of these things assist memory.

As another consequence of oral transmission of knowledge, what was considered worth knowing would change drastically. There'd be no room for catchy tunes, empty jingles, or cute jokes. Like the person going camping or backpacking, what you carried would have to serve more than one function. Stories would be perpetuated in your family and community because they were useful in keeping your sense of family alive, and because they fill important functions.

Your family history would be more than a weight around the neck of your children, more than a harmless diversion or a hobby for retirement; it would be vital in maintaining a place for your family in the community. The story that you told of your family, and that others told about you, would be the knowledge that defined you as a family. Importantly, the stories would be *about* your origins and *about* your activities, but more importantly, the stories would *constitute* you as a family. In other words, the stories would give you existence. No story, no family.

Scientific Proof vs. Narrative Fidelity

Anyone who has ever brought a prospective mate home to meet his or her family knows how embarrassing the moment can be. If yours is like most families, they tell funny stories about growing up. While it may seem like your siblings are just tormenting you (and in my case, I *knew* they were doing it deliberately—but then, so did I!), what they are doing is vital. The stories, which will be told in varying versions for every prospective new family member, define and locate you as a community.

The stories and memories are what make you a family far more than heredity or marriage, and to rehearse them does two things: it re-establishes the identity and space of the family, and it initiates the new member into what it means to be this family. In other words, the stories are a way of auditioning the prospective new member. They declare, "This is who we are as a family," and they ask, "Can you enter into the meaning of this family through these stories, and can you be a part of the ongoing relationships that these stories create?" If the prospective mate can enter the family, only a short time will pass before the family will be including a story or two about them as a way of claiming them as part of the ongoing community.

It's also important to understand that we evaluate family stories by a very different standard than we would use for other types of stories. Have you noticed that in your family, the question whether one of the stories actually *happened* exactly as remembered is seldom asked?

That's because we treat these stories very differently than we'd treat something we expect to be historically accurate, like a newspaper story. We seldom ask, "Is it actually, scientifically true?" That is, can it be proven by any sort of record besides memory and hearsay? Instead, we assess whether the story is *truthful*; that is, if it's consistent with how characters in this family might act under those circumstances. If the story we're hearing doesn't seem consistent, we question it. We test the story, not for objective truth but for what storytellers refer to as "narrative fidelity." What we really want to know is if the story is useful, not if the story is true.

Have you ever wondered why none of the New Testament writers questioned whether the Genesis account of Creation and the Fall was historically true? It's because they didn't have the mental capacity to distinguish between "scientific" proof and narrative fidelity. In simpler terms, Paul used the story to make important points about the relationship of Christ and the church, but he didn't ask if the story was actually true.

Because Paul was addressing oral thinkers, the question would have made no sense. When we argue about whether or not the Genesis account is "true," we mean "Is it provable?" That kind of objective truth is the result of the invention of science in the seventeenth and eighteenth centuries, and for Paul to ask that question is about as meaningful as the apostles arguing over how much time one should microwave popcorn! Without the concepts of popcorn, instant, and electricity leading to the microwave, the question would have simply been madness.

Instead, Paul (and the next several centuries of thinkers) used the story as one that was truthful; that is, it accurately described our place in the universe. The story told us how we came into existence, how God intended for us to relate to Him, the cause of our broken relationship with Him and the rest of creation, our weakness toward temptation, our need for a redeemer, God's grace in planning for reconciliation, and even our tendency to blame our errors on someone else. Whether the event actually occurred exactly as handed down was less important than that the story told us vital things about ourselves. The retelling of the story was necessary, for without it, we had no place in the universe, and the ministry of Jesus would have been of little consequence.

As you can see from these examples, the differences between a world with writing and a world without writing would be drastic. In the modern world, patterned and shaped through the literate mind, we see language as a way of speaking about the world around us. But the location, the sources, and the standards of knowledge, truth, and community are not located in the language we speak. For an oral culture, speaking is a way of ordering, structuring, and recreating the community and its collective wisdom. The things mentioned above—memory, the location and source of knowledge, the ways of transmitting and remembering knowledge, and the function of stories and the standards of truth applied to stories—give language an immensely powerful role in the world.

This chapter explores some of the basic distinctions between a world of orality and the more familiar and comfortable world of literacy. We will compare two casts of mind: the oral and the literate. Later on, we'll look at several Scripture passages in the light of the distinction. What we will find is that the Word, spoken to people who were primarily oral, has peculiar resonance for oral cultures. As members of a literate culture (some would argue that we are post-literate), we can never fully grasp how these verses would reverberate for an oral thinker who heard them proclaimed, but we can understand some of what they would have experienced.

While it would never be possible to rejoin those living in the land of the oral, we can become tourists for a few days. Like the sense of history many experience when standing in the streets of Old Jerusalem, we can pursue our understanding of the Word of God by visiting the world of the oral thinkers who first spoke the mind of God.

Scholars have studied the differences in the mental worlds of orality and literacy for about fifty years, but what those differences mean for non-scholars is what we seek to understand. Perhaps the two most well-known early scholars in the field of orality are Walter Ong and Marshall

McLuhan.* Ong drew on works from literary critics to examine the differences between orality and literacy in historical texts, while McLuhan addressed the questions in terms of new media technologies. While Ong is best known for bringing together a great deal of scattered material from psychology, sociology, classical studies, and theology, McLuhan was more interested in applying the differences to new technologies. Both, however, brought to the table the questions, "How do new technologies affect human thought?" and "How did the invention of writing alter the ways that people experience themselves and their world?"

In this chapter, we'll chart the mental terrain of the two modes of thought. To do so, we'll use Ong's terms to describe differences between oral thinkers ("primary orality") and literate thinkers ("primary literacy"). It may strike readers that computer technology has created a third mode of thought that is much more like orality than literacy, but that depends on writing for its reproduction. That, in part, is what both critics suggested: that we are seeing a return to orality ("secondary orality") that has profound consequences for knowledge. That return to the oral has profound implications for how believers might share their faith in a post-literate world.

Orality in Pre-Literate Cultures

In the days before written texts, the storyteller occupied a central role in his culture. I say *his* because storytellers, so far as we know, were men. While we most often think of storytellers today as entertainers, we do recognize that they occupy other important roles in society. We understand that storytellers preserve a heritage of storytelling. Some specialize in stories that pass on cultural meanings, while others focus on stories that present us with an experience that we find hard to

---

*   *Orality and Literacy* and *The Presence of the Word*. McLuhan wrote *Understanding Media.*Walter J. Ong, *Orality and Literacy: The Technologizing of the Word*. New York: Routledge, 1988.

understand intellectually. Others simply revel in the sheer delight of oral wordplay. But by recognizing and supporting these storytellers, we share in the understanding that they are an essential part of any culture. Most often, we regard storytellers as part of the childhood experience—a way of passing on important knowledge to those who aren't at the point of reading.

For oral cultures, the storyteller occupied an important role indeed (this is not to say that oral cultures no longer exist; they do, but for this book we'll be looking at historical oral cultures particularly). Not only were they entertainers, but also teachers, preservers of knowledge, historians, and shapers of people's reality. The role of storyteller usually combined a connection with the spiritual along with the collective wisdom of the group. The storyteller was perhaps the most important role in such a society, for while the head of the group might be able to direct the actions of the group, only the storyteller could supply *why* the group should continue its efforts to survive.

Since most stories ultimately explain where the community came from, and what its purpose was for existing, the storyteller was often a combination of historian, entertainer, teacher, visionary, and holy man. The first efforts to write stories occurred within a narrow range of years depending on the particular culture, but most of the great myths and stories were first written down around 800 BCE.

Perhaps the best way to describe the thought world in which the storyteller functioned is to say that it was a world of sound. The oral cast of mind emphasized sound over sight, and the oral thinker experienced the world as sounds occurring in time. Oral thinkers tended to live within rhythmic patterns that were tied to the natural, where one moment flowed into the next, without those moments being broken up into separate moments. The changing of the seasons didn't mark the passage of a year that began on a single day and flowed toward an ending, but each season melded into the next. Day passed into night without a sharp change from one to the other; weeks didn't begin on one day and move toward the ending, but each week moved into the next smoothly and seamlessly. In fact, it wasn't until the invention of the calendar several hundred years after 800 BCE that the concept of a "week" became meaningful.

The oral mind understood time more as a circle than as a straight line, where days, weeks, months, and seasons came, fulfilled themselves, and passed into the next without abrupt changes. The oral thinker thus experienced life as a flow of events within a continuous cycle, with few surprises and no departures. Because events were often experienced as a repetition of previous events, oral cultures emphasized the traditional and the communal, and lived by conservatism that would seem positively stifling to a literate thinker.

The role of myth was to pass on what had always worked, to preserve the ways of the community, and thus, to validate the community's existence. The stories themselves emphasize continuity and longevity, rather than innovation and creativity. The Old Testament sensitivity to the intergenerational effects of sin and righteousness was an example of the lingering effects of this view of time, for oral thinkers could easily understand that the consequences of their actions would set in motion patterns that succeeding generations would be bound to emulate.

Oral thinkers were attuned to the community, and took their identity from their place in that community. Because they were rooted in a world of sound, the metaphors used to describe their world were largely of sound rather than sight. It may be puzzling to think of the "voice of God" walking with Adam and Eve in the garden of Eden, and then to think of them hiding from that voice, but if your world is tuned to sound, you tend to describe it in corresponding language.

As a way of illustrating this (notice how choosing to write this encourages me to use visual metaphors: an *illustration* can be seen, not heard, and a *focus* is for the eyes), think of how difficult it is for you to *write* about a *sound*. Now try the opposite challenge: try to explain a sight using only verbal terms. Would metaphors like *focus* make any sense? Can you talk about "illustrating" a sound?

Another way to illustrate this might be more familiar to those of us in long-term relationships. My wife, Theresa, is an artist, while I'm a professor of communication and a musician. We're very different people, and if you spoke with us at length, you might notice a distinct difference in the kinds of words we use to express ourselves. Theresa uses metaphors that are rooted in sight, while I use metaphors that are most often rooted in sound. So, while I might ask, "How does that sound?" Theresa would be more likely to say, "How does that look?" To me, things "sound okay" or "don't sound right," and if I'm trying to help a friend find a job, I'll "keep my ears open and let you know if I hear of anybody looking for help." For Theresa, things "look good" or "don't look right," and if she offers to help the job-hunting friend, she'll "keep her eyes open and let you know if I see openings."

Part of this difference may be due to personal style, but a lot of it comes from the fact that we encounter the world in radically different ways. My world is a world of sounds that take place in time, while Theresa's world is one of visual stimulation. She is fascinated by texture, line, color, contrast, and visual beauty, while I'm fascinated by coordinated sounds in time…so that I'll be as swept away by a piece of beautiful music or a joke told with impeccable timing as Theresa would be by a perfect sunset.

This difference between sight and sound shows up in many other ways—for instance, in our reaction to the other's sensory experience. We both revel in our own sensory world, but prolonged exposure to the other's not only saturates us, it puts us to sleep. I enjoy freeform jazz, which to me is a fascinating exploration of sounds, harmonies, dissonance, and rhythm. Theresa tries to listen, but after a few moments, her senses become so overloaded that she starts yawning. Meanwhile, I'm driving faster because I'm charged up.

On the other hand, I have a tough time in a shopping mall—not because I dislike shopping, but because I can't spend more than twenty minutes in the riot of colors, mirrors, objects, bright signs, and strange shapes that the mall presents to my eyes. For a time, we lived within one hundred miles of some of the best art museums in the country. We were less than three hours from Pittsburgh, Philadelphia, Washington, DC, and Baltimore, and four hours from New York City, and we visited every major museum in the region. I've fallen asleep on benches in some of the most prestigious museums in the world!

But perhaps more important than the difference in sensory overload points is how the different ways of experiencing the world have two different levels of involvement. The world of sound uses more than just the auditory mechanism in isolation. Since sounds occurring in time are really vibrations, the aural person is often more caught up in experiencing, since vibrations are sensed by more than just the ears.

When I turn on the music good and loud, I hear it, but I also feel it in every part of my body. My toes tingle, my hands sense the vibration of the other surfaces in the room, and I find it hard not to move along with the music—even in very subtle ways like tapping my toes. Anybody who has turned on a tape of children's songs in a roomful of children can understand that listening is a full-body experience. In fact, like those children, the more fully I feel and respond to the music, the more fully I experience it. Moving in rhythm to the music only adds to the experience, and the more I move, the richer it becomes.

I'm sure you've gone to a concert, or seen a performance on television, where the musicians move in dramatic ways as they play their instruments. It may almost look like a slow dance with the piano or violin. Musicians don't do that because they are "performing," but because they've moved beyond the notes on the score (which are written) to the physical experience of the music. For accomplished musicians, the notes on the page are tracks of sound, which come alive as the musician's physical movement produces them. They can't help it, since it is their whole body and mind together that are producing the music.

The aural world of music is not passive, or still, or even mental. It's a full-body, physical experience, and hearing it is a physical experience as well. That's why a live concert is so much more exciting than settling back in your armchair to listen to a CD of the same performance, and why we're willing to pay to go see a live concert.

In comparison, the world of sight is radically different. Sight encourages *stillness* rather than movement, and control of physical response rather than physical involvement. In fact, sight encourages the opposite of movement—it encourages not *embracing* the sight, but a very distinct mental distance.

Again, a comparison helps. You've probably had the experience of visiting a museum and seeing a family with children come through. How easy is it for the young children to properly experience the museum? The museum is a place to go and quietly look, but not touch—and it certainly isn't a place to go and wiggle. So we could say that the proper museum experience (at least in museums not dedicated to children) involves not just the *absence* of the other senses, but the *disciplining* of them.

By discipline, we don't mean that literate thinkers are well behaved. We do mean that literate thinkers learn to control parts of their being in order to experience the museum properly. In fact, some thinkers argue that we do more than discipline; we deny the existence and validity of the parts of our being, namely our emotions.

So, in effect, learning to think in a literate fashion involves splitting the self into parts and denying some natural parts of our being. We learn to be reserved, to hold back, to pretend that we're cool and unruffled about everything. This splitting of the self leads to a number of psychological problems that oral thinkers never face. In short, the world of literacy is one of control, not celebration. That's why the oral world was one of dancing and feasting, while our present literate world seems to be one of self-discipline, introspection, and social judgment.

One way we can hear the oral world echoed in the Bible is to examine how divine direction is addressed. I was recently talking with a high school graduate who was concerned about finding the will of God for her future. Angie desired that God would show her His direction, that her focus on Him would be unwavering, and that she would be able to see what would be the correct choice of college. She asked for prayer that no distractions would cause her to lose sight of her goal, and that she wouldn't look to the right or left, but that her vision of the future would be unclouded.

Notice that all of Angie's metaphors were visual. The will of God consists of a vision, a clear goal that must remain unobstructed, and so forth. Now think back to the Old Testament descriptions of finding God's will. The voice of God walked in the garden. David says, "Your ears shall hear a word behind you, saying, 'This is the way, walk in it'" (Isaiah 30:21 NKJV). The Psalms are full of expressions of David's desire to know God more fully, but in most verses, it is the voice that David most desires to understand—not vision. His experience of God comes not through his reading of written works, but through his interaction with the voice that comes to him on the hillside where he tends the sheep as a youth.

When David praises, it is his voice that he asks be heard—"Hear my voice, O Lord," and when he cries in supplication, it's his cry of anguish that he wants heard. Psalm 29 is a good example of David's oral experience of God:

> Give unto the Lord, O ye mighty, give unto the Lord glory and strength. Give unto the Lord the glory due unto his name; worship the Lord in the beauty of holiness. The voice of the Lord is upon the waters: the God of glory thundereth: the Lord is upon many waters. The voice of the Lord is powerful; the voice of the Lord is full of majesty. The voice of the Lord breaketh the cedars; yea, the Lord breaketh the cedars of Lebanon. He maketh them also to skip like a calf; Lebanon and Sirion

like a young unicorn. The voice of the LORD divideth the flames of fire. The voice of the LORD shaketh the wilderness; the LORD shaketh the wilderness of Kadesh. The voice of the LORD maketh the hinds to calve, and discovereth the forests: and in his temple doth every one speak of his glory. The LORD sitteth upon the flood; yea, the LORD sitteth King forever. The LORD will give strength unto his people; the LORD will bless his people with peace.

When David names specific attributes of God for worship, he most often describes the power of God's voice in action. The voice is full of majesty, breaks the cedars, and divides the flames of fire. The understanding of God that David resonates (we won't say "reflects") is very similar to that of Genesis, where it is the voice of God that creates the cosmos through the act of speaking. For oral thinkers, power is inseparable from word, and can only be unleashed through the act of speaking. The power of God does not exist outside of its articulation, and therefore God is always speaking to and over creation.

Notice in Psalm 29 that God *speaking* causes the animals to bring forth their young, a process that we would simply attribute to nature. David says that the best response to the continual speaking of God is for His people to speak of His glory. When David says to give unto the Lord glory and strength, he speaks as an oral thinker, since glory can only be attributed by others and then only as long as His people continue to speak it. The relationship between God and His people depends on the lifting of voices. Both on the human side of speaking glory and praise and on the divine side of holding the universe in balance through continual articulation of power, the voice is essential. For the voice to be silent is far worse than to be overrun by one's enemies.

Psalm 77 echoes the depth of despair from which David cries, but also gives us some indications of how the oral mind manifests itself:

> I cried unto God with my voice, even unto God with my voice; and he gave ear unto me. In the day of my trouble I sought the Lord: my sore ran in the night, and ceased not: my soul refused to be comforted. I remembered God, and was troubled: I complained, and my spirit was overwhelmed. Selah. Thou holdest mine eyes waking: I am so troubled that I cannot speak. I have considered the days of old, the years of ancient times. I call to remembrance my song in the night: I commune with mine own heart: and my spirit made diligent search. Will the Lord cast off for ever? and will he be favourable no more? Is his mercy clean gone for ever? doth his promise fail for evermore? Hath God forgotten to be gracious? hath he in anger shut up his tender mercies? Selah.

David clearly treats this like a conversation in which he expects to be heard as well as to hear. He begins by saying, "I cried to God with my voice," and then immediately repeats the phrase, identifying whom he has cried unto: "even unto God with my voice." The oral mind, which must depend on memory rather than writing, tends to repeat phrases, while adding information each time. Read the first sentence aloud, and notice how the repetition of the first phrase sets up an expectation that is filled by the final phrase "and he gave ear unto me."

Notice also that the first two phrases consist of eight syllables, while the third phrase is seven syllables. This triple phrase construction is typical of oral storytelling formulas. The second sentence consists of three phrases of ten, nine, and nine syllables. Again, it's rhythmic, and the second phrase is an elaboration of the first, with the final phrase completing the thought.

But the most telling feature is how David expresses the depth of his despair: he remembers, he complains, and he becomes so troubled that he finally says he can no longer speak. We might first treat this as hyperbole (exaggeration for the sake of effect) since he then says a lot more. But for the oral thinker, to be rendered speechless by despair—so troubled that you can't speak of your difficulty—is to be cut off from the flow of speech between God and himself. It is, in short, to be helpless. As long as he can cry, as long as he can speak it, he has hope. Take away his voice and his influence, and access to God is gone. You can be so awestruck that you are speechless, so paralyzed by fear that you cannot talk, but those too are moments when you are helpless.

Not only is the oral world one of sound, but, as we've seen with David's psalm, rhythm is heavily emphasized as well. Because repetition and rhythm aid memory, oral thinkers tend to organize what they know through the use of song, saying, and other patterns. We literate thinkers are not so removed from this part of our past. Studies of perception show that we tend to notice what is rhythmic in our environment over things that are not rhythmic. When confronted with data that is continuous and unfamiliar, our minds will often impose some familiar rhythm upon it.

If I asked how many days there are in July, could you tell me without first singing or counting on your knuckles? We probably don't sing aloud unless we're in second grade, but our best way of remembering how many days there are in each month comes through simple songs we learned in grade school. When you're digging through your file drawer, do you find yourself thinking the ABC song? All of these are examples of how we still rely on orally transmitted and organized knowledge for the useful, day-to-day things we deal with. Oral thinkers differ in that they pass on the bulk of their knowledge in this manner.

To summarize this section, let's turn our attention (a visual metaphor) to the oral world's treatment of time. Oral thinkers live in a world of sound and rhythm, while literate thinkers live in a world of sight and linearity. For us in the modern world, time moves in a straight line from left to right. Events are clustered along that line, and are visually fixed, while we are detached and distanced from them.

Oral thinkers live in the present moment, which is characterized by the full experience of taste, sound, feeling, and movement. Literate thought is full of visual metaphors that refer to thought itself—we focus, we seek enlightenment, we want things to be clear, we examine. New ideas appear to be true, while we witness significant events. Our world is not one of taste, feeling, and experiencing the moment, but of discrete moments. Time consists of chunks determined by technologies: our days are carved up into seconds, minutes, and hours, which requires us to think of time as something existing on clocks. Days become weeks with sharp distinctions between each day, while weeks become months and years that are visually depicted on calendars. We even celebrate the beginning and ending of each year.

Since we see time as moving in a straight line, with identifiable beginnings and endings, identifying those beginnings and endings becomes far more crucial to us than they would to an oral thinker. We are driven to discover those discrete points with an intensity that would seem obsessive to an oral thinker, and then we fight to defend them. For instance, we explain the existence of the world in terms of a beginning point—either Creation or a Big Bang—and then go to incredible lengths to justify our chosen view.

Not only is time linear, but it's teleological as well. We see time as beginning from a single point, and then proceeding to an end that is somehow predetermined by the system in which time is embedded. If we are religious, we see time beginning at Creation, and then we see a progressive revelation of God's grace and mercy that was in the mind of God from the very beginning. Time proceeds toward a judgment, at which point eternity begins. The whole thing is planned, and the end result—a new creation in Christ Jesus—is in the mind of God from the very inception. Although it seems different, the scientific view has the same pattern. Life begins with a Big Bang and leads to the evolution of the human being at the top of the chain. Although the two explanations differ, they both see time moving in a straight line, with a predetermined ending.

Think of how this might sound to the oral mind. When does one day end and another begin? We can tell the difference between light and dark, but what is the dividing line without a clock? When does one week and another begin? In fact, at what time should I begin work and at what time should I begin leisure? What divides one month from another? One season from another? Oral thinkers can tell the difference between night and day, and season to season. They could tell what part of the year it was by the holidays and feasts that marked important events. But without calendars (a way of organizing time visually, with sharp beginnings and endings), there is no sense of time proceeding in a line. Rather, time moves in a cycle of days melding into nights, seasons into seasons, and years into years.

Since time for literate thinkers is linear and discrete, we learn to think and speak of time as if it were an object. We talk of saving time, spending time, killing time, or trading time. We distinguish between good time and bad time (quality time or wasted time.) We speak of time as if it were money, and in fact, we often tell each other that time *is* money. For the oral thinker, nothing could be more absurd than the notion that time is like an object that can be spent or saved.

All of these metaphors suggest that we think of time as something within our control—that we can cheat, save, or spend. But the oral thinker would say that we are caught up in the inexorable grip of time, and our culture would encourage us to be at peace with the changes that time brings. The way that a literate thinker deals with the passing of time and the unavoidable phenomenon of aging is to defer acceptance until the early forties. Ironically, we even determine the proper moment for this to happen. We are surprised when it happens ten years earlier or later than we've scheduled it.

Oral cultures treated aging very differently for two reasons. First, oral cultures tended to have shorter life expectancies, and second, everything in oral culture taught people not to fight time in an effort to control it. To oral thinkers, time simply couldn't be controlled or manipulated by human effort, and wisdom came from experience, which could only be attained through the passage of time. Second, the aged held the collective knowledge of the community in their heads. The aged were revered and respected in oral cultures, in contrast to literate cultures, which emphasize what's new, young, and novel. The oral thinker is controlled by time, swept along by its flow, and measured by its continual return.

Tension Between Two Worlds

1. Have you ever been so emotionally stressed that you can't put your feelings into words? What are those experiences like? Are they all bad, or can they be good? What is the connection between emotional experience and the words to express them?

2. Is there a difference between silent prayer (thinking to the Lord and letting Him read our minds) and verbal prayer for the psalmist?

3. In I Samuel 1:9–16. Hannah's silent prayer is so unusual that Samuel misunderstands it and rebukes her for drunkenness. Hannah explains that her silence is because of the depth of her grief. What other biblical examples are there where silence equates to being powerless?

4. In Romans 8:27, Paul says that the Spirit makes intercession for us, with groanings that can't be uttered. How does this relate to the inability to speak and helplessness?

5. Does time move in a line for you, or is it a circle? Is it both at the same time? How do we reconcile the sense that time moves in both a circle and a line?

6. Storytellers are invaluable in an oral world. Who are the storytellers in our current digital world? Do they serve the same function?

7. Think of the metaphors you use to describe experience. Are they visual? Or aural? How would your teaching be different if you replaced your visual metaphors with aural? (For example, "moving forward," "looking to the future," or "making progress"?)

3
Living in an Oral World

Not only does time flow in a circle, but it always returns to its starting point without a hitch. We literate thinkers say that time rushes past us, from behind, and races into the future. Time not only moves in straight vectors, it moves from left to right: from Sunday on the left side of the calendar to Saturday on the right, and from top to bottom. Over longer time periods, we literate thinkers regard the past as being behind us, and the future as being in front, and we walk, moving forward, looking for visual cues to guide us and confirm our choices.

The notion of progress is that we've moved from the starting point, toward our end, and are ahead of others. We're pleased if we judge ourselves to be farther along than we thought we'd be, and especially excited if we're farther along than others. This is one reason we feel that we need to be leading. Every business is leading their field, every person must be a leader, and every expert we quote is a leading scientist. To follow is to be a failure. It's a tragedy if our nation doesn't lead the world in the production of whatever category or widget we care to measure.

The past is left behind us, contained in the records that are preserved in writing. We remember very little, since we don't need to remember—we can always go back and look it up. One of the earliest critics of writing, Socrates, argued that writing results in atrophy of the memory, and he was right. There's even a difference in where the past is contained. For us older folks, the past is written and stored on dusty shelves, always available to go back and recover. For those born in the digital age, the records exist in digital or cloud format. Why remember when you can google it? Why expend the resources to memorize, when instant access to the internet is always on your wrist?

Our minds are not loaded down with useless information, because we have access in digital form at any moment. Facts, figures, and histories can be recalled at any time, any place, in any argument. We're like cyclists on a cross-country trip, with a chase vehicle carrying our baggage: our extra clothes, parts, tents, food, and tools—everything we need. But since oral cultures didn't write their important stories down, they had to carry all of their knowledge with them like baggage. They depended on story, song, and collections of wisdom statements as their knowledge base, and they didn't have room for what they didn't need. In short, they carried only the essentials, not the abstract.

Oral cultures were dedicated to tradition over novelty, and the goal was to pass along the wisdom that was known rather than discovery of the new. Thus, oral cultures tended to be more concerned with preservation of knowledge and the slow inclusion of new experience without rejecting the old. Oral thinkers tended to be non-analytical and uncritical in their thought processes, while it takes literacy to ask the question, "What is the meaning of meaning?"

Before our children were born, Theresa and I liked to vacation and travel by motorcycle. We took several trips from the Midwest to tour the East Coast, carrying only our clothing and gear on the motorcycle. We had a saddle bag on each side, and a square trunk mounted above the rear fender in the back. Because the trunk was the highest point on the back, we could only store light things in it so not to upset the balance of the bike. We used the trunk for helmets, jackets, reading material, and rain suits. We each had a saddle bag the size of a gym bag for our luggage. Imagine taking a ten-day trip with only a small gym bag for your extra clothing. We packed an extra pair of jeans, T-shirts, a sweat-shirt, socks, and maybe a swimsuit. We'd stop at a laundromat every third day to do a load of wash, then be on our way. We learned to live with very little for a short time, and to focus on preservation and main-taining what we carried.

Oral thinkers are much like that. They can only really know what they remember, and so they only remember what they really need. There's no room for batting averages, draft picks, TikToks, or Kardashians in an oral mind. But the oral sensibility had a way of compressing and access-ing knowledge that made it easy to remember what they needed: song and verse. The oral mind is far more capable of remembering than the literate mind, especially if the knowledge is useful and memorable.

To illustrate, I had classes in college that studied lectures in theories of language and eloquence by eighteenth-century teachers. In colonial times, professors would lecture, and students would listen without tak-ing notes, and then later, write out verbatim what they remembered from the lectures. After they finished school, students would have the lecture notes bound as books for their personal library. Many of those libraries were donated to universities by families; thus, there are a lot of copies of Hugh Blair's Harvard lectures on eloquence written by Blair's students.

If you examined several copies of student notes written over a twen-ty-year time span, you would find that they were nearly identical. There were differences in occasional pronouns, or the odd confusion of sim-ilar-sounding words, but they will be close enough to have been tran-scribed from the same event. These young boys (for they were invariably boys between the ages of twelve and fifteen) had listened to two-hour lectures and later written them down almost flawlessly. That tells us two things: first, even as late as the eighteenth century, people's memories were far more developed than today, and second, their teachers never changed their lectures over twenty years. But the pace of discovery was much slower than today, where a new discovery is often obsolete by the time it's published through the traditional peer-review method.

So like backpackers carrying everything with them, oral cultures moved around the circle of time, keeping their cultures alive through song, verse, aphorisms, and festival.

The Evocative Nature of Sound

I vividly remember one special moment of my youth. It was late summer, and I was going into my senior year of high school. One warm, sunny day in late August, I was on my way home from football practice. The windows were down on my '65 Mustang and the radio was blaring. The wind blew in, redolent with the scent of pine trees, freshly cut grass, drying hay, and summer leaves just before they start to turn. Sunlight streamed through the trees alongside the narrow country road, dappling the pavement in front of me.

On the seat next to me was a letter inviting me to visit the college I was interested in attending for the course of study I thought I might pursue. My car was paid for, and I had half a tank of gas and $10 in my pocket—enough to cover dinner and a movie with a date that evening. I had a plan, a path, and a purpose, as well as the richness of feeling like I had everything I needed.

In that moment, I felt, for the first time, that I truly belonged in the universe. It was as if the universe had neatly split into two halves, like a peeled orange, nestled in the palm of my hand. I knew who I was, what I wanted to do, and how to get there. I can't describe the moment completely, but it was a beautiful instance of completeness, discovery, and harmony that brought a lump to my throat and tears to my eyes. And at that moment, for the very first time, through the tinny six-by-nine-inch speaker on my car's back shelf, I heard Barry Manilow singing the song "Mandy."

I never grew to particularly like Barry Manilow (in fact, I think he should have gone directly from "Copacabana" to the elevator without muddying up my listening pleasure). But to this day, whenever I hear that song, I'm transported back to that moment. The sights, the sounds, the smells, the feeling of wind on my face, the sense of completeness, is all evoked by the first strains of music. It still brings tears to my eyes. I've sniffed on a lot of elevators in my day. (I tell younger people that they'll know their day has passed when they hear their prom song on an elevator.)

But here's my point: I can smell freshly cut hay on a summer day, and I'm fine. I can feel the warm wind on my face in August when I drive with the top down, and I'm dry-eyed. I can have the same $10 in my pocket and a piece of good news on the seat beside me, and I'm not affected. But no matter where I am or what I'm doing, it's the sound that evokes and brings together the richness of all those other senses, and, for just a moment, brings the experience back around the circle of time. That's how sound works, and it's in that sense of the power of sound that oral cultures move through time.

My wife recently went through chemotherapy, and part of her recovery during each round was to listen to music and podcasts as she rested. They were encouraging and helpful at the time. Now, months later, she finds the same voices and songs to be depressing and irritating. They remind her of the lowest point of her physical endurance, and evoke the same feelings of nausea, weakness, and helplessness that she felt at her low points. Even though she drank herbal tea and clear soda and ate chicken soup during those episodes, the tastes and smells of tea and soda don't evoke the feelings to the same degree that sound does. She can read the same books, but they don't prompt the same feelings. It's the sound that evokes the entire nexus of experience.

The process of reading is completely different from the immersive experience of hearing. Reading is about conveying specific bits of information without any confusion or any ambiguity. We might say that the whole process of learning to read is that of eliminating input from our other senses.

Remember what it's like reading stories to a young child? We say, "Sit down here with me. Stop wiggling. Stop fidgeting. Stop singing. Look at these pictures and listen only to my voice." Reading is about disciplining ourselves to eliminate wiggling and concentrate on the words on the page. Eventually we learn to not even hear words but to look at the marks on the page and convert them back to the impression of mental sounds. All of this takes concentration and, most of all, disciplining of the body. Some theorists go so far as to say that the process of learning to read *is* the process of disciplining the body, by eliminating all other parts of experience.

Songs are completely different. While reading is about eliminating all sensory experience except sight, song plunges us into a full sensory experience. A song is heard through more than the ears. Song is heard through every part of the body, since sound is a vibration. Although the modern tendency is to write didactic songs, there's still an experiential component that is evocative. Classic hymns, written to teach theology to those who couldn't read, still evoke a sense of awe, majesty, or reverence.

In the process of converting sound to an object, words in the air in time to marks on a page, one goal is to eliminate uncertainty. We are taught to write sentences that are clear, concise, and to the point, and that convey specific bits of information. Writing is about eliminating uncertainty, conveying only what we want to convey, and leading the reader to our conclusion. We are taught that good writing is not about evoking experience, or about generating new ways of thinking and seeing. It's about telling our story and our story alone. Creative writing is different, but few of us use writing creatively.

This is in marked distinction to what we see and hear in Scripture. Go to the book of Proverbs. Proverbs is one of those collections of wisdom statements that oral culture used to preserve and convey knowledge. For instance, Proverbs 8 starts out by asking what wisdom says:

Does not wisdom call out? Does not understanding raise
her voice? At the highest point along the way, where the
paths meet, she takes her stand; beside the gate leading
into the city, at the entrance, she cries aloud: "To you,
O people, I call out; I raise my voice to all mankind. You
who are simple, gain prudence; you who are foolish, set
your hearts on it. Listen, for I have trustworthy things
to say; I open my lips to speak what is right. My mouth
speaks what is true, for my lips detest wickedness. All
the words of my mouth are just; none of them is crooked or perverse. To the discerning all of them are right;
they are upright to those who have found knowledge.
Choose my instruction instead of silver, knowledge
rather than choice gold, for wisdom is more precious
than rubies, and nothing you desire can compare with
her. (vv. 1–11 NIV)

Notice how nothing in this passage would suggest writing? Listen
to the first verse. "Does not wisdom call out? Does not understanding
raise her voice?" Wisdom speaks as a person, conveying truth and life to
a listener as she speaks. Learning is never done in isolation, apart from
the realities of life. It always takes two people to learn, one to speak
and one to hear, and truth comes through the ear rather than the eye.
The one who speaks does so out of concern and love, and the one who
hears isn't passive. Proverbs 18:1 says, "The mind of the prudent acquires
knowledge, and the ear of the wise seeks out knowledge" (NASB). The
hearer *seeks* knowledge in action, not passive reflection.

We see the same regard for learning repeated in Acts, where Philip
meets the official in the Ethiopian court:

And the angel of the Lord spake unto Philip, saying, Arise,
and go toward the south unto the way that goeth down

> from Jerusalem unto Gaza, which is desert. And he arose and went: and, behold, a man of Ethiopia, an eunuch of great authority under Candace queen of the Ethiopians, who had the charge of all her treasure, and had come to Jerusalem for to worship, Was returning, and sitting in the chariot read Esaias the prophet. Then the Spirit said unto Philip, Go near, and join thyself to this chariot. And Philip ran thither to him, and heard him read the prophet Esaias, and said Understandest thou what thou readest? And he said, How can I, except some man should guide me? And he desired Philip that he would come up and sit with him. (Acts 8:26–31)

This man knows how to read because reading is crucial to the job of managing the queen's treasury. But reading isn't how he learns. Reading to him is a tool to perform his job, and when he reads, he speaks the words out loud. He treats what's on the page as the tracks of sound, which must be converted from the page back to sound and spoken to be understood. Even then, when asked if he understood what he read, he doesn't say no. He asks if it's even *possible* to understand without another person there to give voice to knowledge.

We hear the same relationship of sight, sound, and wisdom in St. Augustine's account of meeting the teacher Ambrose, one of the wisest men of his day, nearly three hundred years later.

Augustine has sought out Ambrose to help him reconcile his Greek education as a rhetorician and philosopher with his newfound Christian faith, and he's had a tough time getting to meet him. Ambrose spent much of his time reading to refresh his mind, but what confirms his reputation as a brilliant scholar is what Augustine first notices: Ambrose's ability to read silently.

But when he was reading, his eye glided over the pages, and his heart searched out the sense, but his voice and tongue were at rest. Ofttimes when we had come (for no man was forbidden to enter, nor was it his wont that any who came should be announced to him), we saw him thus reading to himself, and never otherwise; and having long sat silent (for who durst intrude on one so intent?) we were fain to depart.*

Augustine postures himself as the humble, seeking student, full of respect and hope for what he will hear. What he finds is a teacher who is so advanced that he can learn without another voice to teach him. Ambrose can read silently.

Imagine saying that today. "I traveled for days to meet this person, because he was so wise and could help me understand Scripture. I wanted to sit with him, and ask him all sorts of questions so that I could hear his wisdom. When I finally got to meet him, I was absolutely blown away. I walked into his office, and there he was, reading without moving his lips! Not just to show off, since he did it all the time. Brilliant!"

My point is that Augustine finds silent reading to be so remarkable that it confirms Ambrose's reputation for brilliance nearly three hundred years after the Gospel accounts were written. If the ability to read silently was so rare as to be remarkable to Augustine, how much more unusual would silent reading have been to Jesus hearers?

What we hear in Proverbs is more than just the literary device of personifying wisdom by having the character speak on her own behalf. We hear important clues about how wisdom functions only in the sound of the voice. Wisdom can be found just in the company of the wise, as the wise speak. It must be sought, and it must be spoken. This is an aphorism—a wisdom statement that's been passed from hearer to hearer,

---

* *Confession of St. Augustine*, chapter 3, https://www.ccel.org/ccel/augustine/confess.vii.iii.html.

from teacher to pupil, for generations. They weren't read in long passages or presented in lectures, but simply stated and then considered and discussed. They were meant to evoke questions, not lock down a narrow and specific meaning.

That's why many of the Proverbs seem to be contradictions. Proverbs 26:4 says "Answer not a fool according to his folly, lest thou also be like unto him,"while Proverbs 26:5 says "Answer a fool according to his folly, lest he be wise in his own conceit." Which one is true? Both, depending on the circumstances, and the hearer learns how and when through discussion and disputation. When Jesus sends the disciples out to minister, He says, "Don't take food, or money, or extra clothes" (Matthew 10:9) while in Luke 22:36, He says, "But now he that hath a purse, let him take it, and likewise his scrip: and he that hath no sword, let him sell his garment, and buy one." Again, which is the truth? Neither and both; circumstances and active discussion give wisdom its voice.

Wisdom, like faith, comes from hearing, and listen to what she says: "Doesn't wisdom *call out*? Doesn't wisdom even cry out? Isn't wisdom trying to get your attention? Isn't it pursuing you?" (paraphrase). This isn't a literary device meant to spice up a text by personifying something abstract. It's not inventing the guise of a person in order to make a reader think about wisdom in a different light. No, this is what a philosopher might say at the beginning of a teaching session, much like a call to worship.

> On top of the heights beside the way, where the paths meet, she takes her stand; beside the gates, at the opening to the city, at the entrance of the doors, she cries out: "To you, people, I call, And my voice is to mankind. You naive ones, understand prudence; and, you fools, understand wisdom! Listen, for I will speak noble things; and the opening of my lips *will reveal* right things. For my

mouth will proclaim truth; and wickedness is an abom-
ination to my lips. (Proverbs 8:2–7 NASB)

Try reading it aloud, and notice how hard it is to do it quietly. Doesn't
this sound like the resume of a good teacher? A marketing piece, shouted
in the marketplace of a city, as the teacher seeks those who are hungry to
learn? Everything in this chapter is a reference to sound. Wisdom calls,
speaks right things, hates wickedness, utters truth, brings blessing and
justice, righteousness and instruction. Nothing is about a written text. It
doesn't say, "Here, read this brochure, you'll learn something." It shouts,
"Listen to me and live!"

The Oral Mind vs. the Literate Mind

Now, let's summarize some of the differences between the oral cast
of mind and the literate one. In an oral culture, and to the oral mind,
time is circular rather than linear. Time moves in a circle, marked by a
gradual movement of one to the next. Day flows into night, into weeks,
and into years, marked by regular events. The sabbath, the phases of
the moon, and the change of seasons gradually happen, the slow death
of one season and the beginning of another. The festival, the anniversary, the calendar of celebration that marks those events, even though
the changes that they mark are gradual. The past is in front of us, kept
fresh and alive by the retelling of the story and the reminder of the
festival. The future lies behind us, unknown and mostly silent, and
although this seems like a small detail, it will become important later
in our discussion.

Scripture frequently tells us about the spatial orientation of people in
parables, and inverting past and future can be an important clue to how
hearers may have understood it. For instance, when Lot's wife looks
back at the city of Sodom, we modern literate thinkers might describe
her action as a metaphor for not leaving the past. But if the future is

behind us, we could understand it as a warning that this city, and all it represents, is *not* part of our future. When Jesus rebukes Peter by saying, "Get thee behind me, Satan" (Matthew 16:23), we could understand this as a warning to put temptation in the past. Inverting the location of past and future could cause us to hear that Jesus will deal with the spirit of the tempter at some point in the future.

Our history is contained in the stories that are told, and our present is the story being told and shared now. Our community is formed not by our founding documents or written creeds, but by the verbal enactment of the stories and the acceptance of the rhetorics of virtue and vice the stories share. Judgment comes not by reference to abstractions, like a law library, but by communal rehearsal of past decisions through the discussion and disputation of judges. We can hear this in Jesus' day, when the judges discussed what to do with the apostles, who were healing and teaching in Jesus' name: "Remember these other examples of people who rose up claiming to be the messiah? How they came to nothing? Leave this alone; if it's of man, it will fail too, but if it's of God, we don't want to oppose it" (Act 5:34-40 paraphrase).

The oral world emphasizes time and finds itself in a continual present. Rhythmic patterns prevail, and metaphors of experience tend to be oral. The literate cast of mind emphasizes space, with linear patterns and attention to sight, and expresses itself through visual metaphors. "Looking forward," "being enlightened," and "I see what you mean" are illustrations of the literate mind. We can see the truth of the matter, and knowledge is revealed from the darkness of uncertainty. All of these are examples of the literate mind as it finds itself in the world.

To the oral mind, time moves in a circle, in a continuous progression of hours, days, seasons, and years. The passage of time is marked by events, and the community is celebrated through the repeated festivals and celebrations. It's critical to understand that oral cultures saw the future *behind* them rather than in front. Direction comes through a voice from behind that speaks a word, not from a goal in front that is seen. Oral cultures listened for the voice of God, not seeking visual signs to the individual, but listening for a familiar voice.

The oral cast of mind emphasizes the traditional and the communal, and manifests itself as conservatism that doesn't reject the past. Rather, it looks to the past for precedent to guide conduct, and finds its authority in the collective wisdom of the aged. The literate cast of mind emphasizes the individual, and whatever isn't bound by tradition. Even the expression "bound by tradition" conveys the notion that tradition is a trap to be escaped. The literate cast of mind shows itself (there's the visual again!) in cosmologies with an interest in historical distance and alienation from the community.

The oral cast of mind tends to be non-analytic and uncritical, while the literate cast of mind tends to be analytical and critical. The oral cast of mind tends to view words as dynamic, living, and powerful. The spoken word is magical, personal, behavioral, and part of physical reality. The spoken word is creative and saturated with full sensory experience, while the literate cast of mind views words as static objects fixed on a page. Words are impersonal, ideal, and abstractions from reality. Words are thought to refer to other words, which refer to other words, which are defined by other words, all on the page, with no final authority to tell us what any of them truly "mean."

The literate cast of mind is obsessed with taking things apart to see why they work, while the oral cast of mind is satisfied by celebrating the whole. The literate cast of mind is obsessed with what things are not, while the oral cast of mind celebrates what is.

The oral relies on personal memory, using formulas, themes, verse, and commonplaces (premade forms of argument and ways to structure knowledge to gain the hearer's assent). These are handed down from generation to generation, with each generation adding to the common wisdom.

So, if I want to argue about what the future might bring, and how we should prepare ourselves, I might use the notion of probability. What has happened in similar circumstances in the past, and how likely is it that it will happen again? We still use commonplaces to structure argument. For instance, the old journalistic standard of "who, what, when, where, why, and how" used to be the formula for a thoroughly written news story. This format still competes with the listicle—a set of numbered facts with pictures, or the repetition of rumor because it's been reported by another web source.

The literate cast of mind relies not on personal memory, but on technological justification over memory. Emphasis is on creativity, novelty, and the latest findings that have been revealed by the efforts of the experts. We venerate discovery, and pin our hopes on what we don't yet know, making our knowledge much more tenuous. The current use of "science-based" policy is one example of a claim to expertise in public discourse.

We might ask what is meant by "science," but that would risk censure, since anything that doesn't come out of science is bad. The notion that science isn't consensus is lost completely. The default attitude of science is doubt, not confidence, and the posture of science is to be skeptical of any claim until it has been rigorously and repeatedly tested. Scientific statements are tentative and hesitant, expressing uncertainty and disbelief. Oral cultures live surrounded by the confidence in what has always been known, while literate, scientific minds live in constant doubt that any statement could possibly be true until tested by the experts.

The oral cast of mind emphasizes group morality and adherence to clearly understood norms. The role of myth is to teach us what those norms are through the stories of others. We learn, we discover, and we experience in groups, especially in the mixing of the elders with the younger as they pass along what is known. The literate cast of mind emphasizes individual discovery of what is true, and assumes that each person has their own truth to which they must be loyal. No one can possibly understand or know another person's truth, but we can share glimpses of it through what we say and do. In short, the oral cast of mind is never alone, while the literate cast of mind is always alone, trapped inside a world of the senses that can never truly be bridged. Stories are told not to unite us, but to shout our own truth into the void.

Finally, the oral cast of mind tends toward extroversion, and is more limited in imagination. What we see is what you are, not what you say you are. We can only see and hear what you do, and your character doesn't exist outside of your actions. We can judge that you've acted wisely, but not that you are wise. Psychosis is external, and is seen in the actions which don't comport with the community, but that can't be explained. Thus, madness isn't always bad. It may be that you are inspired by a muse in your storytelling, or that you are moved upon by an external force that makes you see the future. Even then, we have a place for you in the community. We watch and listen while you invoke the muse before telling the story, or we seek you out when we want guidance from the oracle.

The literate cast of mind tends toward introversion and free imagination. Psychosis is internal, stemming from the failure to integrate a fractured self somewhere along the line in the process of individuation. Or psychosis is a chemical imbalance in the function of the brain, or possibly stems from exposure to a chemical or contaminant during the gestation process. It may be from exposure to environmental contaminants during early childhood, or may even have genetic origins that are peculiar to a person's heritage. In any case, all of these explanations regard it to be internal and peculiar to the individual.

Orality, Time, and Scripture

"The wise man is the only one who sees what is in front and what is
behind."

—Homer, *The Odyssey*

"Not seeing what is here nor what is behind."

—Sophocles, *Oedipus the King*

If the notion of the past being behind us and the future in front of
us comes from the way our minds have been trained by reading to see
the world, what of it? How is that important? What difference would it
make? We have a past to forget and overcome, a future to imagine and
yearn for, and a present to live in right now. Except that we don't really
have a present. We have the mental trick of calling the moment where
the past and the future come together our present.

As soon as we pick a moment and call it "now," it's passed behind
us into the past. There is no present, only the collision of past and
future. Not so for the oral thinker, who lived in the circle of time, in
the rhythm of the seasons, in the symphony of sensory experience trig-
gered by sounds. We can come close with a handful of holidays, which
present returning stories that we share across our culture. Christmas,
for instance, comes every year. We have rituals, programs, dinners, customs, foods, music, and observances that most of us share, easily evoked
by the sounds of a Christmas carol. Even those who disdain religious
observance are part of the story; they're the ones who provide the plot
for the holiday movies that reassure us each year that it's all part of a
grand story.

If we listen carefully, we can hear this inversion of past and future in
many places in Scripture.

And though the Lord give you the bread of adversity, and the water of affliction, yet shall not thy teachers be removed into a corner any more, but thine eyes shall see thy teachers: And thine ears shall hear a word behind thee, saying, This is the way, walk ye in it, when ye turn to the right hand, and when ye turn to the left. (Isaiah 30:20–21)

Note here that the Lord's promise to Israel is that they would indeed see their teachers, but the voice of wisdom, instruction, direction, and inspiration would come from *behind* them, in the future. Seeing was for the present, the short term, but the actual direction came from behind as a voice.

Thou hast beset me behind and before, and laid thine hand upon me. Such knowledge is too wonderful for me; it is high, I cannot attain unto it. Whither shall I go from thy spirit? Or whither shall I flee from thy presence?" (Psalm 139:5–7)

Here, the psalmist confesses that the Lord's presence is in front of and behind him, and there's no place he can flee that God's presence hasn't already been. The mercy and goodness of the Lord is behind him, in the future, as he sings in Psalm 23:6: "Surely goodness and mercy shall follow me all the days of my life: and I will dwell in the house of the Lord forever." The light unto his feet only shows the next step, and the lamp unto his path in the darkness only shows a feeble glow that quickly fades. But the voice of the Lord is sure, and it is where the singer of praise places his confidence.

We hear the same thing in Ezekiel, who begins one of his prophetic warnings by saying, "Then the spirit took me up, and I heard behind me a voice of a great rushing, saying, Blessed be the glory of the Lord from this place" (3:12). His prophecy is of the future, and the voice that speaks it to him is behind him.

Hundreds of years later, Jesus often referred to the primacy of voice over sight, hearing over writing. He tells His listeners that an evil and adulterous generation seeks a sign, while "My sheep hear my voice...neither shall any man pluck them out of my hand" (John 10:27–28). People can be fooled by what they see, but Christ's followers, who know His voice, won't be misled.

We hear Him place the future behind Him when Jesus is telling His disciples about His coming death, and Peter tries to correct Him:

> And he began to teach them, that the Son of man must suffer many things, and be rejected of the elders, and of the chief priests, and scribes, and be killed, and after three days rise again. And he spake that saying openly. And Peter took him, and began to rebuke him. But when he had turned about and looked on his disciples, he rebuked Peter, saying, Get thee behind me, Satan. (Mark 8:31–33)

One of the most complete New Testament instances that shows us how sight, sound, hearing, writing, past, present, and future come together for a late oral thinker is in Revelation 1:9–19 (NIV):

> I, John, your brother and companion in the suffering and kingdom and patient endurance that are ours in Jesus, was on the island of Patmos because of the word of God and the testimony of Jesus. On the Lord's Day I was in the Spirit, and I heard behind me a loud voice like a trumpet, which said: "Write on a scroll what you see and send it to the seven churches: to Ephesus, Smyrna, Pergamum, Thyatira, Sardis, Philadelphia and Laodicea." I

turned around to see the voice that was speaking to me. And when I turned I saw seven golden lampstands, and among the lampstands was someone like a son of man, dressed in a robe reaching down to his feet and with a golden sash around his chest. The hair on his head was white like wool, as white as snow, and his eyes were like blazing fire. His feet were like bronze glowing in a furnace, and his voice was like the sound of rushing waters. In his right hand he held seven stars, and coming out of his mouth was a sharp, double-edged sword. His face was like the sun shining in all its brilliance. When I saw him, I fell at his feet as though dead. Then he placed his right hand on me and said: "Do not be afraid. I am the First and the Last. I am the Living One; I was dead, and now look, I am alive for ever and ever! And I hold the keys of death and Hades. "Write, therefore, what you have seen, what is now and what will take place later. The mystery of the seven stars that you saw in my right hand and of the seven golden lampstands is this: The seven stars are the angels of the seven churches, and the seven lampstands are the seven churches.

Although John writes what he sees, and that becomes the book of Revelation, it's the future that he sees when he turns. John places the future behind him, and the voice that speaks to him about the future is behind him. He turns, sees what is coming, and records it in writing by dictating it to a scribe, but is completely unable to understand what he sees and writes. When John asks for meaning, the explanation by voice brings comfort, order, and meaning. To each church, John is commanded to write a message of hope, instruction, encouragement, or chastisement, but the message to each church concludes by saying, "He who hath an ear, let him hear what the Spirit saith unto the churches" (Revelation 3:6). They were to be read out loud to each church.

So if the oral, first-century listener inverted the past and future, and saw themselves as looking backward in the big picture, would that change anything for us in the twenty-first century? I would suggest this: Anytime you see a reference in Scripture to "behind and before," stop, go back, and read it as if the past and future were inverted. Speak it aloud, while placing the future behind and the past in front of you. If it makes a difference, keep it. If not, forget about it. In many instances, it will make your understanding of the passage a little bit richer. In some instances, it may differ from the traditional meanings we find in commentary, or even help explain something that's not quite clear.

Do we see the same inversion of past and future in Paul's letters, which serve as the foundation for much of our systematic theology? Paul is one of the most prolific authors in the New Testament. He's a Roman citizen, educated in both the Greek system of his day and the Judaic tradition of his fathers. Paul is trained in the classical rhetoric of his day, drawing on Socrates, Plato, Aristotle, and Cicero, among others. We can clearly see this in his argumentation, his appeals, and his many references to contemporary philosophers. The fact that he can go to Mars Hill and even converse with the professional philosophers of his day shows how well he was trained.

In some instances in his letters, he even seems to be taking on the thinkers of his day in extended refutation. For instance, Aristotle described the virtuous character as being composed of nine elements, which were defined and bound by law and community expectation. Paul described the Christian character in terms of nine fruit, which grow out of the surrender of the heart to the Spirit of God. Paul bookends his list by noting that there is no law that can define or limit the natural display of God's character. The fruit Aristotle describes are remarkably similar to Paul's list, but Paul finds his in surrender to God rather than obedience to human law and expectation.

The point and purpose of a Greek education at that time was to produce a *rhetor*—a well-trained citizen orator who would exercise his citizenship through civic engagement. Every part of the trivium was designed to produce a thinker who could recognize what was needed, formulate an argument about what should be done, and present it to his council using appropriate forms and appeals that would resonate with his hearers. The heart of instruction was rhetoric, the ability to match idea and strategy to situation and audience expectation, and to speak it boldly and well. All the other subjects were there to help create appeals—science to create illustrations, math to assess and demonstrate probabilities, and philosophy to furnish structure. All of this was verbal, not written.

Paul was reticent about his background, but there's much we can infer. He was born in Tarsus, a Roman city, and held citizenship while retaining his Jewish heritage. He was born into a family of means, who could at least afford to send him to Jerusalem for an education, where he studied under Gamaliel in a synagogue school. We don't know if he studied formally, but he was familiar enough with Roman citizenship to use his status as a citizen to gain a hearing before a crowd, and once to secure his release from jail. We can see the marks of his education in the letters that he dictated, both in the way he formulates arguments and in the subjects he addresses.

One of the major issues among thinkers in Paul's day was whether writing stripped what was recorded of its truth. The philosophical tradition of Plato and Socrates thought that since the written word couldn't be questioned and couldn't speak for itself, it could no longer claim to be truth. It might be the written tracks of what someone said they believed to be true, but it couldn't be held as truth. Since the writer wasn't needed any longer, the only thing the philosopher could depend on was the written text, which gave no indication of how it was to be read. Irony, hyperbole, sarcasm, and any of the other aural cues that would tell the reader how to hear the voice of the writer, were all missing. All of those came from tone, cadence, and other cues that we now call non-verbal, which could be inferred by the reader but never confirmed by the text.

Others held that writing was more accurate than oral teaching, as it was exact, edited, and portable. In some cases it was shorter. But since it was dictated to a scribe, writing held most of the marks of the oral method of composition and delivery. Many of our current transitions echo ancient ways of remembering what one planned to say. A common mnemonic device was to associate each point with a room in the speaker's house. To call a point to memory, one simply took a mental stroll through the house, retrieving each point along the way. "In the first place" and "in the second place" referred to places that were associated with ideas.

One indication that Paul was steeped in the oral tradition was the way he started his letters by addressing the question of the power of the spoken word over the written. In every one of his letters, he begins by saying he has no ability to speak, but that it's the foolishness of preaching that saves. He comes down on the side of oral declaration over written exploration of truth. It is important to note that he does his best work when he's writing to believers in Roman university towns—centers of learning and disputation where the questions about writing, speaking, and truth were one of the most hotly contested topics in the academy.

A lot of effort has been expended by scholars to identify Paul's thorn in the flesh, and many of the biographies of Paul contain some reference to a speech impediment of some kind. But another way to understand Paul's frequent reference to his inability to speak well is to understand that the first thing required of a speaker in the oral tradition is to disclaim any ability to speak. This is to put the audience at ease, and to set aside the question of pride distorting good advice. By denying the ability to speak well, the speaker was demonstrating recognition of what the hearers needed to be reassured. They were inviting a positive judgment of their message by demonstrating humility and sensitivity. The Greeks termed this *ethos*—the invitation of a positive judgment about the speaker's character, which would then argue for the truth of the speaker's message.

One of the most complete and extensive versions of this is found in Job 32, which is itself all about speaking truth. Elihu was the youngest of Job's friends, and he begins his remarks thus:

> I am young in years and you are old; therefore I was shy
> and afraid to tell you what I think. I thought age should
> speak, and increased years should teach wisdom. But it is
> spirit in man, and the breath of the Almighty gives them
> understanding. The abundant in years may not be wise,
> nor may elders understand justice. So I say, Listen to me,
> I too will tell what I think. (vv. 6–10 NASB)

Elihu spends the next thirty verses explaining why he's not really qualified because he's young and inexperienced, but that the spirit in him is ready to burst if he doesn't share what little wisdom he has about Job's plight. Circumstances, the situation, the inability of the others to come to a sound conclusion, and Job's desperation call for him to speak. It's not up to him; it just has to be said.

Past, Present, and Paul

In his letter to the Philippians, Paul tells us how he regards the past and the future:

> That I may know him, and the power of his resurrection,
> and the fellowship of his sufferings, being made con-
> formable unto his death; if by any means I might attain
> unto the resurrection of the dead. Not as though I had
> already attained, either were already perfect: but I follow
> after, if that I may apprehend that for which also I am

> apprehended of Christ Jesus. Brethren, I count not myself
> to have apprehended: but *this* one thing *I do*, forgetting
> those things which are behind, and reaching forth unto
> those things which are before, I press toward the mark
> for the prize of the high calling of God in Christ Jesus. Let
> us therefore, as many as be perfect, be thus minded: and
> if in any thing ye be otherwise minded, God shall reveal
> even this unto you. (Philippians 3:10–15)

Modern readers would find the phrase "that I may apprehend that for which I am apprehended of Christ Jesus" awkward to read in any translation. But oral listeners, more attuned to the rhythms of the spoken word, would most likely have heard an allusion to Jacob wrestling the angel in Genesis 32.

To set the story, Jacob is returning to his home after decades of estrangement from his brother. With his mother's help, he had tricked his father out of his older brother Esau's birthright. Jacob has been chastened, disciplined, and greatly blessed by God over the years of exile, but he doesn't know what will happen when he returns home to face his older brother. Jacob has sent his wives, children, servants, cattle, sheep, and belongings ahead while he has stayed behind, and there, an angel stops him and seizes him. In the strength of desperation, Jacob wrestles with the angel to escape, until he realizes who this is; then he holds on. The angel demands to be released, and Jacob refuses, even sustaining a permanent injury to his hip. Jacob refuses to let go until he has been blessed. He names the place Pennial, for he says it is there that he has seen the face of God.

When Paul says he wants to get ahold of God for the very purpose God has gotten ahold of him, it's easy to get bogged down in complex sentence structures and abstractions. But we can hear the same desperation and conviction in Paul's voice as we hear in Jacob: "Everything that I have, no matter how great it is, is nothing compared to what I really want—to know Him, and the power of His resurrection. He knocked me to the ground in the middle of the desert, blinded me, then restored my sight. He inverted my understanding of who I was fighting against. Now I want to grab ahold of Him for the same reason He grabbed ahold of me. I don't count myself to have done it, but here's how I try: forgetting what lies behind, and reaching for what lies ahead, I press toward the mark" (Philippians 3:8–14 paraphrase).

How often have we heard it taught that Paul is saying he forgets his past, and strains for the future, and by doing this, he can struggle toward the mark for the prize of the high calling of God in Christ Jesus? Further, Paul admonishes anyone who is mature to be of the same mind—to think and live the same way. But is this what an oral audience would hear? We know that less than 3 percent of the population could read and write at that time, and scholars of literacy and orality insist that primary orality persisted until the early eighteenth century. Even then, the shift to literacy was gradual and tenuous, taking until the early 1940s before universal literacy became a goal of education.

But we hear it everywhere: "You have to forget your past. Overcome your past. Don't dwell on the past. Don't let your past define you. Don't let your past ruin your future. Move fast so your past doesn't catch up." We're taught to forget our past and look to the future in every facet of our lives.

What if Paul, an oral thinker, dictating a letter to a scribe to be read aloud to an oral-thinking church audience, thinks of the past differently than modern thinkers? What if, true to oral culture, the audience hears the exact opposite? If our past is in front of us, kept alive as the present through song, story, ritual, remembrance, and celebration, and our future is behind us, unknown and unknowable, wouldn't we hear it differently? That we should forget the future, and hold on to our past, and by celebrating that past, *back* into the future? Listening for a voice of guidance rather than seeking a sign? What if this call is to cast all thought about the future coming behind us, and to hold on to our history, our heritage, and our faith by telling the story of how He transformed us? To take no thought for the morrow, because today has enough trouble of its own?

Wherever he goes, and whatever audience he addresses, Paul tells his story. True, he counts some elements of it as rubbish. He counts the things that impress his peers as garbage, but he doesn't stop telling those parts because the redemption of those parts *is* the story of his salvation! Paul judges them to be rubbish, not worth speaking about, but then he never stops talking about them. If he truly meant to leave his past behind him, wouldn't he have to stop telling the story?

Learned Discontent

I believe that much of our modern-day discontent and frustration is because we've been taught to understand Paul's statement with a twenty-first-century literate mind. For us, the past is an obstacle to overcome, an embarrassment to us, or a painful but necessary steppingstone to what we now hope we are. But this is the product of literacy.

For the oral thinker, the past was not an obstacle to be overcome, or an anchor holding us back and preventing us from becoming all God wants us to be. It was not a failure or an embarrassment that threatened to catch up to us and drag us down. The past is really the playground of God's mercy and grace. It's all we have, and it's the place of our story— what He's done, the liberty and favor we've received as a result, and the hope we have for whatever comes next. But we're taught by nearly every book, song, sermon, and story to try to forget the past, while trying to make sense of who we are.

Just this morning, while driving, I heard the local Christian radio DJ talk about his word for the year: *forgetting*. He spoke at length about forgetting the past year, blocking it out of his memory, and living as if the disruptions of 2020 had never happened. But this presents a conundrum: We don't want to forget the good things that God has done, so we sift through our past, trying to decide what to keep and what to bury. But this makes us judges of God's activity in our life. It's as if we are baseball umpires, calling balls and strikes on the King of the universe's pitches. Or like we're rummaging through our sock drawer, like Marie Kondo, keeping what brings us joy and throwing out what we remember with pain or sorrow. But every new encounter or piece of information can change our judgment; even not getting enough sleep can make us dismiss whole episodes of life as "not good enough."

I believe that one of the biggest sources of discontentment and disappointment can be found when we become judges of God's handiwork. How can I be disappointed unless I'm first appointed to something I didn't get? How can I be disillusioned unless I'm first illusioned? Teaching us to forget our past while holding to our testimony is a contradiction, because it forces us to make judgments about God's ways and purposes. "That's a strike. Good pitch, God! Ball one. Just missed the outside corner, Lord!"

We invent clever and sophisticated ways to do this. For instance, we come up with the notion that God *wanted* this experience, but He *allowed* that one. This one was to make me a better person, or that one was because I screwed up. This one was because God was teaching me something; that one was because of my stubbornness. Do you sense how sifting through our past asks us to sit in judgment of His handiwork? How divided that makes us? How unstable? How do we decide what to keep and what to bury, and by what standards do we decide what parts of our past are good and worth keeping? How do we decide that what the Lord brought us into or through is good enough for us?

My first business failure happened when I was nineteen. My real estate sales career was crushed by a recession that spiked interest rates to 18 percent, if money could be found. I took the only job I could find, in an iron foundry, making drainage grates and underground utility vault covers. I stayed with that company for seven years, until I was downsized from a corporate position that I had been moved into after four years in production management. Seven years almost to the day from when I walked into the place, I was standing on a curb in the parking lot with my wilted plant under one arm and a shoebox with a coffee cup and a few pictures under the other, wondering what just happened.

Did all of that make me a better person? I have no clue. I can't judge God's pathways. Did God teach me something? Again, no clue, but I learned a great deal about His faithfulness to provide shelter and food during a famine. I learned much about promotion—that it doesn't come from hard work and determination and goal setting plus a little of God; promotion comes from the Lord. Did it hurt? Greatly. I felt totally rejected. Would I forget it, or drop it from my history once I'd gotten over feeling like I'd failed? Never!

It's an important part of my story, but at the end of the day, the biggest part of His plan was that I met and occasionally ministered to many people I never would have met otherwise. I never would have become friends with many of the people I met there. I learned that if we take His presence wherever we go, that simply by showing up, we change the wrong situation into the right time and place for whomever we meet in those circumstances. That although the King of the universe owns everything and is present everywhere, an important part of what He does is through others. I'm still discovering things from those years, and as we face economic uncertainty once again, I'm bolstered by the knowledge that He can provide. Through the past four recessions, He has provided, but never in the same way, and I'm still learning how those seven years fit into the story of my life.

Over the years, other efforts have come up short, from companies, to charities, to colleges, to ministries. Each time, beyond the disappointment, God has had another assignment once the dust has settled. Each time, He has moved me into a group of people that I wasn't thinking about and, in some cases, didn't even know existed. In each new situation, I met people whose lives were eternally changed by God's hand. I can celebrate those failures because they never were failures. They were changes of assignment, and the people that were affected are never the same. Their generations are forever changed, because the Lord changed the assignment.

We all have the same calling—to be conformed to the image of His Son, to show forth His glory, and to share His mercy and grace with whoever crosses our paths. Where we live out this calling is an assignment, and assignments change over time. How we enter and exit the assignment is a matter of wisdom and following God's leading. In some cases, changes of assignment are obvious; the company closes and you lose your job. In others, it isn't so obvious, and we need to rely more heavily on prayer and the counsel of trusted friends to hear the voice of leading. But when we leave, we leave behind seed that may take years to sprout, and we may never know that the seeds sprouted.

Now, you may be asking, "Doesn't Paul say that everything in his past is rubbish? Isn't he rejecting his past and focusing on his future? What about his metaphor of a footrace, where the runner has to look ahead to the finish line? Isn't that putting the future in front of him?" Not really. He says it's all rubbish compared to what he now has: the knowledge of the grace of God. The change that God has made in him, and the way the change happened, become key parts of the story that he tells over and over. He has learned to take no thought for the morrow. Paul is complete and content, the two things we've taught ourselves never to be.

Instead of rejecting his past, Paul makes the contrast between his prior life and his current life through rebirth the center of his story. He allows the past, and the way that God changed him, to define who he is, and he never stops telling that story. He tells it to paupers and kings, wealthy business owners like Lydia and fishermen on the island of Crete. He tells it to anyone who will listen, and in so doing, he uses the comparison between what he thought he wanted, and what he received through mercy and grace, to rise to the top.

While he also uses the metaphor of the prize at the end of a race, his listeners wouldn't have heard that as putting the future in front of him. A race happens in the present, and the finish line is in the present. Our sense of past and present may be unstable, but even we wouldn't look at the finish line of a race, ten seconds away, and see it as the future. Even a marathon happens in the present, and we don't see every mile covered as fading into the past. So one can use the race metaphor, and see the finish line ahead, without living in the literate sense of time.

I'm writing this on January 15, and the YMCA parking lot is still filled with cars as I drive by. It probably won't be full in another month. In spite of the COVID pandemic and lockdowns, gym membership and use are up at this time of year. We've just passed New Year's Day, which is the day each year when we raise dissatisfaction to an art form. We tell ourselves that our lives aren't good enough, and that we need to change something about ourselves, whether it's losing weight, spending less time on our phones, or even doing something we'd like to do but always put off. In another month, we'll settle back into our normal routines, and the gym parking lot will slowly revert to a ghost town.

I stopped making New Year's resolutions a long time ago, for several reasons. First, a resolution is based on what I imagine myself to be instead of how God sees me. That's a distortion from the very beginning. I can't see myself clearly, nor can I see the things that He wants to change unless He shows me. If I pick something to eliminate because of my distorted view of perfection from comparing myself to celebrities, it may be the very part of my personality that He wants to use. If, like Paul, the life I now lead is by the grace and mercy of God, and He directs my steps and knows my personality from the womb, how can I weigh up my life and decide what needs to go or stay? What causes me embarrassment and what causes me joy?

Resolutions come out of what I imagine my life is supposed to be like, instead of what I am, and what I am is clear only to the One who redeemed me. I'm not saying that everything happens for a reason and someday we'll know it. I'm saying that every episode of life, and every facet of my personality and character, is determined by the One who made me and now directs my steps. How then can I determine my way, if I can only see what I think is worth seeing? My future is even less clear and certain. What I imagine my future to be never comes to pass, no matter how badly I want it. Every scenario I dream up is just that—a path that God never takes.

But what about goals? What about dreams? Go ahead and make them. Go ahead and dream them. They'll never happen as you dream them, and the outcomes will never be what you envision them to be. Just as we may never see the fruit of what we sow on this side of the dirt, we can never see what God has in store for us. As the proverb says, how can man direct his way if he doesn't know what's in his own heart? We may occasionally be graced by God with a glimpse of what He wants to do, but in my experience, they're fragments only, and there's never a sense of how it will happen. From a contrarian's point of view, if you can set a goal and plan out how to get there, it's not God, and He's not obligated to see it through.

In addition to comparing my imperfect view of myself to a fictional future view of myself, resolutions also come out of comparing myself to others. We're inundated by comparisons to others. I don't mean in terms of classic advertising, which always told us that we were incomplete unless we had what the person in the ad has. I mean direct comparison of ourselves to an average. Just look at the headlines on your home page. "How much money you should have saved for retirement? How old are you? Here's how much money should you have." Or, "How tall are you? Here's what should you weigh." Or, "Here are ten things you're doing wrong when you cook an omelet." Or, "What shape is your face? Here are ten styles of eyeglasses to avoid." And on and on. All comparisons of ourselves to the lives of others.

Even the statistical grounding of the social justice movement is comparison, and the passion for social justice is supported not by compassion, but by the dissatisfaction that comes from comparison. "What ethnicity are you? Here's how much money you make compared to that ethnicity." "What gender are you? Here's how much more that gender makes on average than you." "What age are you? Here's how much money you should have compared to people that age."

To be clear, I'm not suggesting that the differences don't exist, or that differences measured by the gathering of statistics are good. But I am saying that statistical measurement is always the comparison of difference, and assuming that any difference is the product of power, and that the exercise of power is always bad, is the product not just of literacy, but literacy of a pernicious kind. It's born out of comparing ourselves to ourselves, and comparing ourselves to others.

In his second letter to the Corinthian church, Paul talks about those who falsely claim apostolic authority:

> For we dare not make ourselves of the number, or compare ourselves with some that commend themselves; but they measuring themselves by themselves, and comparing themselves among themselves, are not wise. (2 Corinthians 10:12)

In short, New Year's resolutions are born out of a comparison of ourselves to ourselves, or comparison of ourselves among ourselves. We compare our imperfect understanding of who we are to an imperfect vision of who we think we want to be, or we compare our imperfect understanding of who we are to who we think others are. And as Paul says, that's not wise.

Comparison and Authenticity

In addition to freezing time and making unwise comparisons, we burden ourselves with the notions of transparency and authenticity. Like many other ideas, these terms are discussed and debated at an academic level, which filters down to the level of popular talk. When they get filtered, they are simplified into bullet points that look good on a PowerPoint slide, and in the reduction, key understandings are lost. Like "holding someone accountable" may mean asking for an explanation and a justification of decisions when used by researchers, but when reduced to a meme, it simply becomes "punish." I suspect that the words mean something else, and the lack of specificity makes them linguistic tofu. They can be used as a substitute for any other ingredient, but never have any flavor themselves. Let's start with authenticity.

When applied to art, music, designer clothing, or any artistic or creative work, authenticity is a useful measurement. An authentic painting is one that was painted by the actual artist, and not a reproduction. This helps establish scarcity, which, combined with desirability, may assist in determining value. Other elements include the cachet of ownership (social capital) and maybe even pleasure in the aesthetic beauty of the object. An authentic painting is one that truly is what it purports to be. Leaving aside the question whether the painter created the entire work, or only supplied the finishing touches and signature in a school setting (a common practice among the European masters), authenticity has to do with whether it's genuine or real.

When communication scholars discuss authenticity, it's far more subtle. They struggle with a shift in our understanding of what communication is, as we become inundated with new technologies. Since the 1940s and the communication model introduced by Claude Shannon, we've come to view communication as a vehicle to convey information. But this is a very new and completely Western view, and a reflection of technology and the application of scientific method to messy human talk. (Later I'll say more about how the Shannon model has influenced our thinking, and how it has permeated all of our teaching about relationships in the church. But for now, let's just say that most cultures and communities throughout history understand communication as something entirely different than a vehicle to convey meaning.)

What we're seeing is the shift from what Ong called "primary literacy" to "secondary orality," which is a short form of literacy presented in an oral stream. In short, we read snippets but they're not stories, like grazing at a buffet instead of sitting down to a formal meal. Our news stories have gone from long discussions of "who, what, when, where, why, and how" to ten photos with captions and a headline. It's food, it's nourishment, but it's much more like grabbing what you can and eating it while standing up.

It's in the postmodern space of unwinding communication, as an information vehicle, that authenticity gets discussed. For instance, this is taken from a journal article entitled "Postmodern Ethics and the Reconstruction of Authenticity in Communication-Based Society."[*]

> Society is represented by a paradigmatic change...we are witnessing a shift from a modern theory of communication as informational vehicle to a postmodern one, of communication as relation. The relational—affective aspect which occupied a central position in the old modern and illuminist concept of communication becomes essential. "The postmodern and globalizing concept of communication considers as a primordial trait not the generation of information but the building of relations. (...) To communicate means to be in a relation because the origin of community lays in the need to relate to other people, to make them cooperate, to coordinate their actions regarding different commune purposes. " The comfortable knowledge episteme is surpassed by the uncomfortably fluid episteme of communication. In this

---

[*]   Grad, Iulia & Sandu, Frunza. (2016). Postmodern ethics and the reconstruction of authenticity in communication-based society. 53. 326-336.

context, "besides the world wide web, the introduction of virtual reality is one of the defining characteristics of the world we live in."

Notice what the authors are asserting here. First, communication is not a vehicle for conveying meaning only, but communication is at the heart of all community, and that to speak is always an act of community building, not just a passive means of conveying message content. Second, the relational and emotional dimension of language is crucial to understanding communication, and that understanding communication as community is primordial; that is, it predates modern understanding that models communication as "sending messages."

In short, our natural state is oral, cultures up until very recently have been oral, and we're reverting back to a pre-literate psychodynamic through the proliferation of online communities. Central to this old understanding is the knowledge that every time we speak, we are building or tearing down, creating or destroying. Authenticity is rooted in the conviction that we are responsible for what we do with words every time we utter them, that what we see of the world is only part, and that our words are always and only an articulation of our experience; they are never "truth" that others must adopt.

This prompts me to ask several questions: First, how close is this to what we mean when we say that we should be authentic? And second, how close is this to what we hear throughout Scripture? Jesus told us that if we commit an act of violence, we are in danger of judgment, but if we call a brother *racca*, which means worthless and without any value, we're in danger of a greater judgment. Perhaps this understanding of the way the voice builds up or destroys is why Paul so often came down on the side of oral proclamation as the power of the gospel.

About ten years ago, I sat through a marriage retreat session on authenticity. The book that the leaders were using to create the sessions modeled "authentic" communication through a theory called the Johari

Window.* This theory describes all communication as emanating from one of four quadrants of self-knowledge. Joe and Harry came up with something that looks like this:

	Known to self	Not known to self
Known to others	Arena	Blind Spot
Not known to others	Façade	Unknown

- What we say can come out of what we know about ourselves and what others know about us. They match up; this is good stuff!
- Some of what we say comes out of what we don't see about ourselves that others see. Blind spot; this is bad stuff!
- Some of what we say comes out of what we know about ourselves that others don't know. This is posing; it is bad stuff!
- Some of what we say comes out of what we, and others, don't know about ourselves. This is confusing; it is bad stuff!

If you want a better marriage, better friendships, to be a better leader, etc., make sure that what you say comes out of what you know about yourself and what others know about you; this is *authentic!*

The Johari Window was devised by Joseph Luft and Harry Ingram in 1955, as a tool for assessing self-awareness in relationships. Through repetition, basic college courses, and self-help and coaching literature, the model's terminology and assumptions have become gospel as a tool to build better relationships. A simple Google search for "Johari" will turn up roughly 1.5 million results. Clicking on one or two will bring you to articles teaching you how to become

---

*   Luft, J; Ingram, H. (1955) "The Johari window, a; graphic model of interpersonal awareness." *Proceedings of the Western Training Laboratory in Group Development.* Los Angeles: University of California, Los Angeles.

a better communicator, leader, business owner, parent, or dog walker by applying the concept of the Johari Window. A simple, descriptive tool to measure and assess self-awareness has passed into the popular mind as the Truth (capital T) about how to be a better person. In construction, this would be like a tape measure becoming the building code inspector.

Just this morning, I opened an email containing a daily devotion that goes out to several hundred thousand subscribers. The verse for the day was Psalm 36:10: "Continue your love to those who know you, your righteousness to the upright in heart" (NIV). Under the title "Do You Know Who You Are?" the author tells us that "years ago a man named Jahari" developed a self-assessment tool help us discover who we are by comparing ourselves to those who know us. Description quickly became prescription: "The transparent life is the life we should desire. I know who I am and others know me. There is nothing hidden. I have come to know who I am as an individual and basically people get what they see in me."*

I'm not trying to bash the devotional, but I share it because it illustrates the way that we've taken simple descriptions from 1950s psychology and made them into tools to explain two-thousand-year-old Scriptures. We repeat what we've been taught in our classes, what we hear in sermons, and what we read in the popular press until it becomes truth. Here, "a man named Jahari" suggests that the insight comes from having it heard enough times to be memorable. But is this what the psalmist had in mind when the songs were first sung? Is this how first-century oral thinkers understood themselves and others? Or has what we think of as the self changed over time?

The Johari Window was embraced by writers about relationships because it seemed clear, concise, and easily taught, and it worked well in a visual diagram. Through repetition by teacher after teacher, the

---

* Hillman, Os. "Do You Know Who You Are? *Today God is First,* 2/11/2022, https://todaygodisfirst.com/os-hillman/

terminology and thinking have gone from explicit to implicit in much of our thinking about relationships. Lest we think that it's only popular literature that relies on the theory, a 2020 doctoral thesis assesses leadership skills and designs leadership skill training for recent seminary graduates based on the Johari Window.[*] But closer examination of some of the assumptions in the model, when compared to Scripture, might make us uncomfortable.

In the marriage seminar, Johari's thinking about relationships was being taught as the key to a strong Christian marriage. First, Scripture tells us that we don't know our own hearts, and that others can't know us or themselves. That's all God's province. Second, this theory is coming from two psychologists who would never acknowledge that we are created in God's image, joined together in a commitment to love and honor one another before God, and fully aware that God alone knows the intentions behind our words. Modeling a Christian marriage on the thinking of those who would deny the very existence of God, and would ridicule the belief itself, is absurd.

Third, the unspoken assumption about communication is that it is a vehicle to send and receive messages, and that authenticity depends on us both getting the same bundle of information. In short, this treats the relationship as a container, and communication as the means to fill it. This theory makes the self pre-eminent over the community, and sees the community arising from the interactions of independent entities. It sees full disclosure as appropriate and desired, marking the difference between "healthy" and "unhealthy" relationships. It sees intimacy as arising from disclosure so that one is honest with themselves. It sees the beginning and end of relationship about yourself, not the other or both.

---

[*] Kratzer, Dustin William. "Developing Additional Leadership Skills of Recent Seminary Graduates in Pastoral Ministry. 2020, https://repository.sbts.edu/bitstream/handle/10392/6120/Kratzer_sbts.pdp_0207A.pdf?sequence=1

In short, Johari defines and describes all relationships as equal, and best defined and understood in therapeutic terms. A biblical view, and actually a postmodern view, would see the relationship resulting from communication, and the shape of the relationship defined by whether the participants were equally committed to honor and respect one another as themselves.

Finally, the term *authenticity* is one of those buzz words that we use as if we all know what it means, when we clearly don't. We can substitute *transparency* and *openness* (both of which come out of Johari's terminology), but those are just as slippery to define. I've heard *transparency* described as holding nothing back; if someone asks you how you're doing, don't lie...being honest with yourself and God, not hiding anything... as if the measure of good communication is based solely on the quantity of what we share. This comes from another model of communication that has been adopted without examination by many Christian authors, and then repeated by busy pastors and teachers who don't have time to dig into the theories behind the popular titles of the month.

Perhaps a big reason that these modern teachings about relationships leave us excited but unfulfilled is because our congregations know that what they're hearing doesn't line up with real life. If orality is primordial, then we are essentially oral beings trapped in a literate mindset. Our heads may be more or less literate, but our hearts are oral and know that saying everything all the time doesn't make stronger relationships. We know, from experience, that there are things we say and things we just don't say, depending on circumstances. We don't disclose everything to strangers when we're face-to-face. We might do it online, but even then, it's very risky. The risk of cancellation for saying the wrong thing ten years ago may just be too great. The notion of authenticity calls for incredible mental gymnastics.

"How are you doing?"

Pause to think. *This is who I am. No, this is who I think I am. But wait, this is who I think I think I am. But this may not be authentic and open, because I clearly understand that I should be something else. I've resolved to be what I think you think I think I should be.* "I'm good."

"Cool."

Contrast that with the way Paul tells his story: "This is where I came from, what shaped me before my encounter with Jesus in the desert. This is how He changed me. It's all His doing, and everything that will come, whether living, dying, being bound, being free, being cold, hungry, naked, or poor, abounding or being abased, is all God's doing. I only know my story of Christ and Him crucified, and what that means for all of us. I don't yearn for a future that I can't attain; I leave that in God's hands and celebrate all that He's done as enough. I forget my future, and I hold onto my past, and I listen for a voice telling me which way is His way."

Let me conclude with this: Let's not live caught between the demands of a past that we think is never good enough to keep, and a future that could never be, unable to even see ourselves in the present as "real." Let's not hang ourselves, crucified between two thieves, or hiding behind the fig leaves of embarrassment. Like Paul and the hearers of his day, let's do this one thing: to lay ahold of Jesus for the same purpose He has when He laid ahold of us. Let's treasure everything He's done every step of the way, celebrating over and over the richness of His grace.

That's how God redeems our past—not by rejecting it or making us pick through it like yesterday's trash, but by making it the central part of a story that will never stop being told. A story that not even the angels are privileged to tell. Let's forget our future, born out of distance, suspicion, and discontent, and listen for the wonderful voice of eternity behind us, whispering, "This. This is the way; walk in it."

Tension Between Two Worlds: Orality and Time

Philippians 3:13 says, "Brethren, I count not myself to have apprehended: but this one thing I do, forgetting those things which are behind, and reaching forth unto those things which are before, I press toward the mark for the prize of the high calling of God in Christ Jesus."

1. How do we reconcile the tension between controlling our lives through planning, and floating through life accepting that the Lord directs our steps?

2. Jesus tells us that anyone who sets out to build without counting the cost is a fool, but He also tells us to take no thought for tomorrow, as the problems of today are enough for us to worry about. How do we do both?

3. How do we reconcile our feelings about our past with our hopes for the future without freezing time and judging God's handiwork? Or can we regard everything as part of His footsteps?

4. How would understanding that we face our past, and listen for direction without trying to control the future, change how we teach about past, present, and future?

5. Do we really need to overcome our past, or reject our past, or rise above our past, if it's what the Lord used to bring us to Him?

6. How can we set goals and aspirations for our futures, without judging ourselves as inadequate or flawed, when we are where we are because of God's activity in our life? If where we are, and where we've been are His leading, can we aspire to change without judging and rejecting God's handiwork?

7. Paul's attitude seems to be "I don't fully understand, but my growth will come from forgetting about my future and celebrating how He's made my story part of our story." How can we incorporate that attitude into everything that we teach?

4

Faithfulness or Success?

The year 1776 marked the origin of two events that shaped the church and its members today. One was the American Revolution, and the other was the publication of a book.

The Wealth of Nations, by Adam Smith, is the seminal work that introduced the theory of free-market economics. Smith's critique of mercantilism asserts that humans have a natural, innate tendency to put our own needs and interests first, so economic systems that give people the opportunity to increase their own wealth will lead to the growth and development of the community's wealth. Smith's argument was the result of talking with leading thinkers and economists for over a decade, so it is not his own singular thought. It's the crystallization of trends and countertrends in economics that had been growing to the point that articulation was important. Smith's work was a statement of what many had been thinking.

While Smith's book is written about economies and countries, it also establishes a key thought that is still current today: that all human activity is motivated by profit, or the desire to see a return on one's investment that can be measured and evaluated. Darwin would later echo the desire to maximize self-interest into his theory of evolution, where the notion of maximizing one's hold in the gene pool becomes the driver of the development of life itself. Much of Smith's thinking was woven into the founding documents that define America's constitutional form of government. Along the way, the idea that all human activity is motivated by profit has become one of the dominant explanations of individual behavior and decision-making.

In the last chapter, we learned how an oral conception of time differs from a literate sense of time, how our modern sense of time is linear and teleological, and how linear time would differ from a circular sense of time. Linear time puts the future ahead and the past behind, makes the present a fiction, and requires us to become judges of the importance of past events. Judging the past in order to decide what to keep and what to forget requires us to freeze time and impose standards of good and bad on experience.

In this chapter, we'll determine whether the standards we use to judge experiences are the same standards that a first-century oral thinker would use. Since Adam Smith's definition of all human activity as profit seeking has become the default for modern thinkers, it shouldn't surprise us that our standards of judgment are very different from what we find in Scripture. The simple fact is that the modern concept of success is not to be found among the oral hearers of biblical times. What we do find in oral cultures is an emphasis on faithfulness and obedience, not profit.

Think of how profit works. I invest or risk this much, and I receive back this much. If I reap more than I sow, it's profit; if I reap less, it's a loss. Gains and losses are measured in terms of whether the return is more or less within our risk tolerance, within our expectation, or what our neighbor gets. If the gain is a lot more than I expected, it's a great success; if it's slightly more than expected, it's a smaller success. Same for loss. It's our expectation that sets the bar, and a discrete measurement that determines profit or loss. But as we should also recognize, this involves comparing ourselves to ourselves, or by ourselves, and makes us judges of whatever results God brings.

But we extend the motive for profit into every area of human activity, and then we end up treating relationships with others in the same fashion. We've learned to treat time as if it were money and it can be measured, saved, kept, invested, wasted, or defeated. We learn to measure the results of how we spend time as if they are profit or loss. We teach ourselves to enter or exit relationships based on whether we think our time is worth it, whether we are getting what we need out of it, or whether we're putting more into it than we're getting out of it. We look at what God is doing in the same way. This can lead to some very strange results.

Back in the later 1980s, my wife and I moved to a university town in the East to start a campus ministry to international students. We went through the first year finding out about our city and learning traffic patterns, locations, rush hours, etc. We met neighbors, settled into new roles as grad students and teaching assistants, met a few people, taught some Bible studies, held small worship meetings, and were absolutely delighted when two of the students decided to be baptized in the late spring of the first year. Oh, and my wife became pregnant with our first miracle child—something that had eluded us during the ten years we'd tried to start a family.

During the late summer, before the start of the second year, we were back in the Midwest visiting family, and I bumped into a local pastor in a bookstore. He asked how things were going, and I excitedly told him that we'd gotten to town, learned where the dry cleaner was, figured out how to navigate traffic patterns, met neighbors, gotten into new roles, and held some Bible studies. And of course, we'd baptized two students. The pastor looked at me with great pity, sincerity, and compassion, and said, "Brother, I'll pray for you that your faith doesn't fail." I asked if he was serious, and he nodded and lugubriously said he hoped the second year would be successful.

I lost a supporter (and burned a bridge) when I responded, "Yes, it's too bad that God screwed up so badly. A whole year, and He's only transformed two people from death to life, only changed the generations of two families for eternity, only made all the angels in heaven rejoice twice. We'll give Him a pass and hope that He'll do better in the future. I'll go back home and apologize on God's behalf to the two students whose lives have been changed." The pastor didn't know what to say.

Another church that supported us wanted to know how many souls we'd won, and what we planned to do in the next few years to raise the total. They were evaluating whether the amount of support we were receiving was justified, compared to what other ministries were doing with similar financial support. Apparently, they had it worked out to a dollar-per-soul-won ratio (DPS), which they used to decide where to put their contributions. I suggested that we hadn't won any souls—God had—and that the ones He had ministered to had taken entire lifetimes to get to where they were.

Besides, the book of James has something to say about those who boast about their plans to go into such and such a city and buy and sell and get gain: "Shut up!" (James 4:13 paraphrase). What we ought to say is that we may live, and if we do, maybe we'll do this or that, but anything beyond that is boasting. We all laughed about it, but my low DPS ratio was probably the reason I was traded the next year for a couple of late draft picks and a minor-league utility outfielder.

The modern notion of success that we use to judge the things of God simply isn't in the Scriptures. We judge something successful when we get back more than we put into it, within the time frame we've set for measurement. The expectation of return is usually a comparison to what we think we, or others, should get back. And as my DPS ratio suggests, the measurement of good or bad is often vague and subjective.

We can trace this back to Smith, but we can also go back much further and suggest the kind of analytical thought and treatment of time as linear traces back to the advent of literacy. Like the notion of progress, which we use to mean that we're further along the path toward an ending than we were the last time we checked, or we're further along the path than others are, success or failure comes out of linear time. Notice how anything that seems to slow down or impede the progress we think we should be making is referred to as "something we're going through"?

The standard for oral cultures is not success; it's faithfulness. Not "Did we get back more than we put in?" but "Did we do what we were required and expected to do?" There's no claiming an omniscient view here, only a focus on the community and authority. Time is not an issue unless there is a season for the action, and everything has a season. Jesus didn't commend people for being successful; He commended them for being faithful. When He asked them to do something unusual, their confidence was displayed by their obedience.

Faithfulness in Action

Recreational fishing is huge in my part of the country, and the story of the disciples fishing (John 21) has special resonance. I think the story contains one of the strongest proofs for the veracity of miracles, just in the way that the story is set. The disciples have fished all night and caught nothing. As they are returning to shore, Jesus appears and yells out over the water, asking if they caught anything. The disciples' answer is no.

That right there is a miracle. Have you ever heard of an honest fisherman? "We were practicing catch and release." "A bear came by and ate them." "An eagle flew over, and you know the rest." "We met a hungry-looking family and gave them all our fish." The disciples' biggest risk was that they would look stupid in front of their peers on the waterfront if they caught nothing, and admitting it only added to their humiliation.

When Jesus told them to fish on the other side of the boat, it could have sounded almost like a joke, or like He was teasing them. But the disciples must have heard the sounds of a command, and despite the fact that it was given by a non-expert, they complied. Again, they were risking a lot of teasing if Jesus were right, and it's likely that anybody watching would have known who Jesus was. But their faith and obedience allowed onlookers to see that Jesus could command something as simple, and as important, as a netful of fish. We moderns don't catch the significance of an empty net at the end of a long day of work, especially since we don't live tomorrow on what we catch today.

There were few job choices in Jesus' day and in most oral cultures. Since the focus was on survival and continuation rather than innovation and progress, most jobs had a direct link to real needs of the community as it stood. Most members of the community were engaged in occupations that satisfied basic needs: shelter, food, clothing, and occasional trade with other communities for things that couldn't be produced locally. Carpentry, food production (hunting, fishing, farming), and, to some extent, merchantry, were the core parts of an oral culture. Storytelling was critical, but this wasn't a role for everyone; it was for the elders and the few who were carefully trained.

Only one of those occupations (trade) could be measured in terms of money spent and money received. The rest worked on faithfulness, and offered little control over outcomes. Planting at the proper time, tending through a growing season, and harvesting when growth was complete and the season was right could be done, but no one could control rain, heat, crop disease, and insect damage. It was a given that the yield would be more than the seed, but the direct link between sowing and reaping wasn't the same as our modern profit motive.

> And he said, So is the kingdom of God, as if a man should cast seed into the ground; And should sleep, and rise night and day, and the seed should spring and grow up, he knoweth not how. (Mark 4:26)

The parable of the sower is unique, in that it's one of the few parables where Jesus tells the disciples what He means. He describes it as being about the hearts of the hearers, but we use it to illustrate all sorts of modern notions about the kingdom of God. I've heard this used to suggest a 25 percent rate of conversion for Bible studies, either as a goal or as a reality ("Don't worry; only one in four give their lives to Christ," or "Work harder; you're only at one in eight"). I've heard sermons about what the modern thorns are for us: our phones, jobs, money, status, possessions. I've heard sermons about soil ratios, how to identify good soil, and all sorts of other numerically based lessons. Our penchant is to screen this through our profit-driven, number-based, control-oriented, and analytical ways of thinking.

As a child, I loved to visit my grandfather's farm. We'd go to a small, rural Methodist church on Sunday morning, and one morning, this parable was discussed in the adult Sunday school class. Most of the members were small farmers, and some of the adults had been born in the 1890s, so while they could read and write, they had been educated decades before literacy became compulsory. They still retained much of an oral sensibility, and, as farmers, they heard an entirely different story. Imagine sending a hired hand out to plant, and when he comes back to the barn at the end of the day, having this conversation:

"How did it go?"

"Pretty well. I got the first bag all planted on the road."

"Ah...anything else?"

"Yup. I got the second bag planted on the gravel driveway."

"Ooookaaay...what else?"

"I got the third bag planted around the rose bushes."

"Hmmm. Did you manage to get any of it on the flat brown area out there?"

"Oh yeah. I got the last bag out there on the dirt."

Can you imagine commending the guy for that kind of day? Then, to top it off, Jesus said the seed sprang up "he knew not how." He had no clue how the act of sowing resulted in any sort of growth. This guy is a knucklehead, to say the least! But he's commended for his faithfulness.

Does this mean that my job is to get crazy, fling seed in all directions, and not care if it grows or not? What about success? Getting back more than I put into it? Making profit? Proving that I'm a good steward by being careful with the seed? Or is it all about faithfulness and obedience regardless of the outcome?

Just like the mental tricks we need to play to judge the past, measuring success takes the same mental tricks. To judge that some effort is a success, we need to freeze time, put sharp beginning and ending points on experience, and hold it up to our flawed measuring stick. And the stick is always personal, seldom due to conditions beyond our control. If the field is barren because of drought, we still blame ourselves for the drought, or if there are parasites, we blame ourselves for the parasites. Our profit-driven thinking causes us to take the credit and the blame for sun, wind, and rain. It's one of the most effective ways we have of loading ourselves down with guilt.

Let me share one of the experiences that helped me learn this.

During my season of working for the foundry, I met a young man about my age who had been hired as a trainee in the sales department. As part of his training, he worked as an inside service rep supporting outside salespeople. We struck up a friendship, and I learned that he had been a student at a Catholic pre-seminary, where he was preparing to enter studies for the priesthood. He'd come from a large family in a small, close-knit Midwestern town, and his family had pointed him toward the priesthood since he was a very young child. The problem was that he had serious questions about his faith, and he wasn't at all sure about what he was supposed to believe and teach others. So he dropped out of college and found a job as a sales trainee.

Since he seemed interested in discussing Scripture, my wife and I invited him to join us in a Bible study, where we talked through a lot of the books he'd read, the questions that had been raised, and the experiences he'd had. He even doubted God's existence, wondered why there was suffering and how we were supposed to overcome our greed and human limitations with something as flimsy as parchment pages. Basic questions about faith, existence, meaning, and purpose. We started at Genesis, and worked through a basic overview of the Old and New Testaments, with some emphasis on philosophical and historical evidence for the veracity of Scripture.

Eventually, we got to the Gospels, and the story of the Passion, and from there, moved on to Paul's experiences and struggles as he sought a mature expression of faith. It was here that our friend stopped us. The Scriptures had been speaking to him, and he realized that if he continued, he'd have to make some serious decisions about his own journey. He'd have to either decide to embrace faith or walk away. In a cold sweat, he said that he simply didn't feel ready to make that decision. "I know where this is going and what comes next—repentance and baptism—and I'm just not ready to let my family down."

I respected that and said I understood, and we stopped our studies and concentrated on our golf games and the occasional lunch, which were just a little bit uncomfortable. Then, a few months later, we went our separate ways—he to a sales territory, and I to the long march out the door with my shoe box under one arm and my plant under the other.

We lost touch after that, and I didn't know what happened to him. I counted the whole thing as a failure, because he'd never committed his life. I filed it all away as one of those "fished all night with no results" episodes—a failure. Every once in a while I'd remember our discussions, say a quick prayer for him, and try to "put it behind me."

Then, almost thirty years later, I was listening to a local Christian radio station as I was driving to an appointment. I heard an announcement by a local church, inviting people to a special service celebrating the church's one-hundredth anniversary. The voice inviting the community to come celebrate with them came from my friend, who introduced himself as the pastor. I grabbed my phone, called the church, and found out that just a few years after we'd gone our separate ways, the Lord had brought him to the point of decision. He'd chosen faith, gone back to college and then seminary, and had been pastor of that church for nearly twenty-five years!

To be sure, there were many people he'd met along the way who had challenged him, mentored him, loved him, and shaped him. He'd been struggling with his faith long before we met, and he didn't simply run out and make up his mind the week after we stopped our Bible studies. He didn't have a dramatic confrontation or some great physical crisis, just a gradual journey that brought him to the point where he was ready to surrender. But our times were instrumental in planting some of the seeds of peace, joy, and confidence in God, and while they weren't the only ones, my fingerprints were on the vessel!

Imagine how it felt to learn, after so long, that the seed had sprung up, that my fingerprints were on his ministry, and that my influence, no matter how small, helped shape multiple generations of believers. That shaping continues today, another ten years later, and will continue for years to come in the young people who were inspired to pursue ministries and missions. Just like in the story of the sower who flung seed in all directions, the seed sprang up with no knowledge of how it happened. In short, we have no idea how the seed we sow impacts others, no idea of the timing, and no idea of the fruit that can come from it. It's never wasted, will never return void, but will always accomplish what it is appointed to do! In light of that, success or failure as a standard of eternal life makes no sense whatsoever.

I believe this kind of thing happens often. We find out seed that was sown years ago has come to fruition, and we weren't even aware of it. A chance remark, an event, or some small kindness makes an impression that God uses to bring about great change. Sometimes it's not even what we said or did, but what the person remembers that God uses. Anyone who has taught the Word for any length of time has had someone tell them that they were deeply affected by something they had said, yet that person won't even remember saying it as part of their sermon.

I was greatly blessed to see the result, but that doesn't mean it hasn't happened before or that it isn't happening with you. I believe that the Lord does this much more than we know, and from time to time He lets us see it. I also believe that heaven may just involve finding out how often God changed people through seed that sprang up we knew not how.

For thirty years, if I had thought about it at all, I judged that Bible study as a failure. My friend had made up his mind to stop where he was, and that was it. I imposed an ending to the Spirit's work, and applied an economic standard to measure the outcome. I'd invested this much time and effort, and only seen an imperfect, incomplete result. I put a period where God put a comma, and ended the story where God started another chapter. I ended the movie walking into the mist, and never thought about the screenshot of the dusty street, with the tumbleweed rolling in the wind and the capitalized, gilt-edged letters saying "30 Years Later..."

Can we take another lesson from the parable of the sower? There are three elements to the sower's actions. First, he obeyed the master and sowed. Second, he didn't prejudge where he sowed the seed based on his flawed understanding of whether it would grow. Third, he had no clue how it grew; he sowed it and didn't think of it again until the master asked.

What if we could think of moments in our life this way? What if instead of asking what kind of seed is in the bag, what kind of soil we should look for, and what's the expected growing season and the expected yield, we simply believed that everything God created has its seed in itself (potential for life), and each seed has its own timing (written in the DNA of the seed)? Once sown, it still needs sun and rain over its time to come to fruition, but that's not up to us. We can pull weeds, throw fertilizer, and chase away the crows, but beyond that, we can only trust God and the natural process of growth.

We have so little to do with the process that it's almost ludicrous. When I drive through the countryside, I see rows of trees marking the end of every field. It's not because farmers left trees when land was cleared; it's often because they built fences, and birds roosted on them. Undigested seeds got dropped under the fence, and since there was nothing to be gained by clearing them, they grew into trees. I'm pretty sure that any bird, in its short lifetime, has planted more trees than I have in all my years!

Sometimes, the seed we sow takes years to grow, and sometimes it happens quickly. That's because the person we meet has been in preparation for years, and we're simply one more in a long line of people God uses to bring about His work. Sometimes, the Lord has been preparing that soil for years, and we just happen to be the one to plant a critical seed. Even then, we may not know that we're doing it until years later. The growth cycle of the plant is in the seed, not in my determination or planning.

The Fateful Burger

This next story begins one Friday evening soon after I had committed my life to Christ. I was with a group of young adults, we had just finished a youth service at church, and we were hungry. About three carloads of us went to a local burger joint for fries and fellowship, but I took a wrong turn and ended up at a different restaurant. Instead of a large group, it was three of us at a table eating fries and solving the problems of the world. Then the door opened, and I watched a familiar person walk in, order, and sit at a table on the other side of the dining room. It was a person I'd known in high school. We hadn't been close friends, but we'd played on the same sports teams and belonged to a few of the same clubs.

During a lull in my table's conversation, I went over to say hello. We traded greetings, and Mike asked me where I was coming from. I briefly but excitedly told him my story while he slowly chewed his burger: how I'd left college after a year because it wasn't fulfilling, and how I'd realized that my hunger for God could only be satisfied by solving the question of what He wanted for my life. I shared the series of chance encounters, events, and circumstances that led me to a Bible study, where I found the start of the answers I was looking for. I told him that I no longer partied or drank, that I was discovering the joy of God's presence, learning His Word, and seeing miraculous things around me.

Mike thought that was all cool but didn't say much else. He told me that he'd been working, getting an apartment, hanging out, and trying to think about what came next. I soon noticed that my friends were getting their things together to leave, so I told him that it was great to see him and that I hoped he'd be blessed. *That was fun*, I thought as I left. *There must have been a reason for our ending up at that particular burger joint by mistake.* Then I promptly forgot the encounter.

About ten years later, my dad invited me to be his guest at a father-son banquet his church was putting on. My relationship with my dad had been kind of rocky over the years, not since we disagreed, but because we were so similar in many ways. And as a young believer with a dynamic experience, my enthusiasm and newfound knowledge wasn't tempered by the wisdom to know when to shut up. So when my dad invited me to the banquet, I was touched and accepted the invitation gratefully. I was also excited to go to the banquet, since it was held at the same small country church where three generations of my family had attended, and where I'd worn out several Sunday school teachers with my juvenile antics.

We had the normal Midwestern church basement dinner of tater-tot casserole, fried chicken, and ground baloney sandwiches, followed by cake. (This was important; nothing that happens in a church is official until cake is eaten. The early believers broke bread, and we ate cake.) Anyway, the evening speaker came in as the meal was winding down, and I was blown away. It was a small group of students from a local martial arts school who were going to talk about using karate to teach and encourage spiritual discipline. The school was run by none other than Mike, the friend I had last seen over a burger and fries on a Friday evening a decade earlier. I was delighted to see him, and eager to hear what he had to share.

After Mike and his team of students were introduced, he began his opening remarks by sharing the story of how he came to faith. He described his high school years of sports and partying, the occasional class, and the sense of fun and camaraderie. He talked about graduating, finding a job, and feeling the emptiness of the long slog of life without a center. He described his fear, depression, and anxiety, and how the combination of partying, drugs, and drinking in a vain effort to fill the emptiness had brought him to the point of contemplating suicide. Finally, he said, he felt that he had reached his end, and with the bottle of pills in his pocket, he had set out. But the last thing he wanted was one more burger from his favorite burger restaurant.

Then, he described walking into the restaurant and seeing an old high school friend with a couple of other kids, looking like they were having the time of their lives. The friend looked very different, and when he came over to say hello, Mike could tell that he wasn't the same person he'd known just a few years earlier. The friend enthusiastically shared his story of hunger, searching, encounter, surrender, and joy, and Mike realized that there might still be answers. He felt a glimmer of hope. So Mike ate his burger, turned around and went back home, and threw his pills away.

He continued his search, only now he prayed for the same kind of life-changing experience that he'd felt when we talked in the restaurant. Over time, Mike met other believers who helped him, and God changed his life. The desire to share his story in order to help change people's lives was motivated by the "chance" encounter he'd had years before that Mike said had saved his life. "I always start my talks with the story of how I came to Christ. But tonight is different, because the friend is sitting right over there."

The sower had no clue how the seed sprang up, and I had no idea that the seed I randomly threw that night had grown into a ministry. I had hardly even known it was a seed. Was it a success? Was it a failure? Did I get back more than I invested? Or was I supposed to throw seed wherever it landed, and go on my way trusting that the seed would do the work God purposed for it? And then rejoice years later when God graciously allowed me to see that the seed had found good soil? What if I had decided to hold back the seed because I didn't understand God's seasons? Or because I made a snap judgment about soil quality and the chances of growth?

In order to make judgments about the success or failure of whatever God brings us, we first need to impose our ending on the episode. That's easy if we think of time as linear, and stories moving from beginning to end in a straight line. But Mike's story, no matter how touching, is a story that could be told by anyone who has been born again. We've all encountered emptiness and hunger; we've all encountered a moment of decision; and we've all made our choices, in part, because someone along the way sowed a seed that God used to bring us to a point of surrender. Sometimes the sower gets to see that something grew, but most times the sower is unaware. Many times, we may not even know that we were sowing anything. And that's as it should be! But the story itself never stops being told by God, over and over again in the lives of His creation.

The Season of Growth

Sometimes the seed grows quickly. This story begins back in the early years of my walk with God. Or maybe, in the circle of time, it began years before when seed was sown into my heart as a young child. No matter. It's the Master who tells the story that gets the glory, who gets to decide the beginning and the ending. Anyway, one of the young men who was part of the circle of friends in my youth group had a high school friend named Dan. He'd come to some of our meetings, fellowshipped with us from time to time, and engaged in some serious discussions about faith and the philosophy course he was taking at the local college campus. Dan was a very careful thinker who wanted to understand what he was doing and why he did it. He was always just a little reserved, but clearly enjoyed the emotional part of our commitment to God.

Dan and I eventually began a Bible study, and as we reached the point in the New Testament book of Acts where the Spirit is poured out on the Day of Pentecost, Dan ended the study. Like my coworker would later say, he knew that he was reaching a point where he'd have to make some serious decisions, and he just wasn't ready. The last thing Dan said before we parted was, "I'm not ready. When I am, I'll let you know, but right now, I'm not ready."

Eight years went by, and during that time Dan was scarce. I'd see him every once in a while at a gas station or in a store, and we'd say hello and chat for a few minutes. But no long conversations, no coffee chats—just a brief greeting and a few comments and gone. I counted all of the time we'd spent earlier as a failure. But then, one Sunday morning, I was preparing for a service. I was leading worship that Sunday, and was praying over my song list and the service in general. I felt a tap on my shoulder, and when I looked up, there was Dan. The first words out of Dan's mouth were, "I'm ready."

"Huh?" I said.

"I said I'd tell you when I was ready, and I'm ready." And was he ever!

Dan gave his life to Christ that morning, and after the service, we decided to resume our Bible study. He was living in an apartment with a younger brother and a friend, and we were going to have the study at his apartment. The first night, he introduced me to his brother Bob, and Bob wanted to sit in. By our third study session, their sister decided to come. She and the man she married became missionaries. Dan's mother came. She gave her life to Christ. And Bob? He's been the pastor of a church in a Chicago suburb for more than twenty years.

I can't begin to quantify how much seed has been sown through that family. And the seed I threw? Just a handful among many, sown over years of interaction with scores of believers—but still part of the story of an untold harvest!

How then can I judge the success or failure of my sowing? Success and failure have nothing to do with what God asks of us, only that we be faithful. Jesus commended His disciples for their faithfulness and willingness to do what He asked, regardless of outcome, and regardless of how silly it may have seemed to them or to others. Jesus often asked the disciples to do the opposite of what was expected: "You've heard this, but I say this" is a common phrase in the Gospels. The Sermon on the Mount is an almost endless set of inversions: "You've heard it said this, but I say this. The law says this, but I say this."

Most of us struggle with the two notions that seem at odds: faithfulness demands action without caring about outcomes, while success requires that I see all of the obstacles and assess the chances that the outcome I want will happen in the time frame I expect. Our culture teaches us success, yet our faith heritage teaches us faithfulness. Our heads are mired in control, while our hearts are anchored in faithfulness.

Often, the two get mixed by well-meaning teachers who try to frame the kingdom in terms of success. We'll take Scriptures that are spoken to the oral cast of mind, and read them through the lens of the literate, and end up with a self-help book that says "here's how to apply this Scripture to achieve this outcome." For instance, the Bible refers to material blessing many times, and if we read through literacy, it's easy to make those Scriptures prescriptive. We'll say, "If God blesses the giver more than the receiver, and if the one who gives gets back more in this life besides the life to come, the key to having more is to give more. If you want to make x, begin tithing on it, because God is obligated to bless the other 90 percent."

So here's the formula for success: Find Scriptures that seem to be about material success, and use them to wrestle God into a corner and make Him do what you want. Our literate mind is all about defining, analyzing, predicting, and controlling, and when we apply this to God, we're bound to feel dissatisfied and discontent. We set ourselves up not only to fail, but to question His love and care for us.

Here's another example of how faithfulness can be the very opposite of the formula of success: praying for our enemy.

Jesus told us to pray for our enemies and for those who mistreat us, and that's a difficult thing to do. We want to justify ourselves, plot revenge, and look for ways to even out the scales. We'll pray for strength to carry on, for grace under pressure, and maybe for God to strike them down or afflict them with malware, but praying for God to *bless* them? How can we bring ourselves to do that? And what if He really does bless them? What happens to us?

The simple fact is that great material wealth can be an opportunity to do great good or, at the other end of the spectrum, a license to be stupid. Few things are scarier than a wealthy person with no sense. God doesn't give us the potential to do great harm or great good unless He first prepares us to be faithful to use His gifts wisely. Otherwise, it would be too easy to use our wealth and leverage to carry out the revenge our flesh demands. How did Jesus learn obedience? Through the things He suffered. I'm suggesting that God doesn't put a weapon in our hands until we're capable of surrendering it to His control. Just as we wouldn't give a sword to a three-year-old, we should understand that the Lord must prepare us to be faithful.

Ah, we think, then my difficulty with that person is because He's teaching me something. Well, yes, it might be that. Or it might be that He'd like to get ahold of that person, and the best way to do it is through hardship. God delights in blessing, and seeks opportunity to bless all of His creation. If we pray that our enemies would be greatly blessed, aren't we asking God to first bring the circumstances that develop maturity and wisdom? Put simply, instead of praying that I be blessed, which He may or may not do, praying for *you* to be blessed may be asking God to bring the very hardship, loss, difficulty, and pain that teaches wisdom. I'm asking for the goodness of God to bring you to repentance, but that goodness involves preparation before it involves receiving. Praying for the person may be asking God to intensify the difficulty in the other person's life.

That doesn't mean my problem will instantly get better. It may make the problem worse. But praying for the enemy releases us to be part of God's purpose. We've all used the illustration of the metal being worked at the forge to describe hardship. We can see several roles for ourselves in the example. Our first thought is that we're the metal being worked. We're being heated in the fire, brought to the anvil, and then hammered into shape with painful but skilled blows. "Hold on," we say, "God is shaping me."

We can also see ourselves (though never as often as we'd like to think) as the one wielding the hammer of the Word, shaping the metal. We're the one bringing the word of correction and instruction into your life, so whale away! We can think of the fire as if it's our affliction or hurt. All of these may be involved, but only if we see *ourselves* as the point of the whole mess. Or we may really be the anvil. We may be the hardened block of metal that the blacksmith is working the heated and softened metal against, and our job is to retain our shape, unyielding and solid, while the Master Craftsman uses the fires of affliction to shape someone else! If we try to measure our efforts in terms of profit or loss, success or failure, we shortchange ourselves and God.

Or take the common sermon illustration of clay being worked on the wheel. All the sermons that I've ever heard using this image from Isaiah focus on *me* as the point of the analogy. All roads lead to *me*, and they usually lead to some message about gritting my teeth and surrendering so the Lord can perfect *me*. To be sure, sometimes it is us on the potter's wheel, but just once, wouldn't it be fun and freeing to find out that we're the table on top of the wheel, spinning in what seems like endless circles, while some other clay gets worked by the Master?

Or take the analogy of the refiner's fire. I could be the metal in the crucible being refined, and seldom bring the word that turns up the heat, but what if I'm the crucible, and it's my backside that's getting flamed so someone else can be purified? Again, my job is to endure without flinching while God does His work on someone else! It's not about me! What I'm really saying here is that affliction and difficulty may not be about us at all, but about others around us who God is trying to reach. Our job is to stay faithful, pray, and bless. And as we grow in maturity, we find that trials and setbacks are seldom about us at all. They're about God doing something in someone else, and using someone next to that person who is willing to remain constant. Rather than a "setback being a setup" for *me*, it's more often a reassignment so that God can work to redeem some other part of His creation.

Success and Unrealistic Expectations

The modern notion of success creates unrealistic expectations, leading us to measure success or failure in terms of what we invested and what we expected to get back within a specific timeframe. We thus judge as failure what is really still growing according to its seasons and God's purpose. Jesus talked about seeds, fruit, and growth often, but He also addressed unrealistic expectations and what might lie behind them. In Luke, He spoke this parable:

> He spake also this parable; a certain man had a fig tree planted in his vineyard; and he came and sought fruit thereon, and found none. Then said he unto the dresser of his vineyard, Behold, these three years I come seeking fruit on this fig tree, and find none: cut it down; why cumbereth it the ground? And he answering said unto him, Lord, let it alone this year also, till I shall dig about

it, and dung it: And if it bear fruit, well: and if not, then
after that thou shalt cut it down. (Luke 13:6–9)

No explanation is given, and Jesus doesn't refer to the parable again.
Obviously, planting a tree and expecting fruit in year one is unreason-
able, and this owner clearly expects more from the tree than any tree can
produce. But in year three, he still doesn't see fruit, and now it seems
reasonable to make the judgment that the effort is a failure. This parable
is often used to illustrate the kindness and care of the vineyard keeper,
who asks for another year for the tree to produce. And that seems like a
more reasonable time frame.

But listen to Leviticus 19:23–25:

> And when ye shall come into the land, and shall have
> planted all manner of trees for food, then ye shall count
> the fruit thereof as uncircumcised; three years shall it be
> as uncircumcised unto you: it shall not be eaten of. But in
> the fourth year all the fruit thereof shall be holy to praise
> the Lord. And in the fifth year shall ye eat of the fruit
> thereof, that it may yield unto you the increase thereof; I
> am the Lord your God.

According to the Law, when they planted fruit trees, they were to
count the fruit as uncircumcised for the first three years. They were to
let it fall to the ground as fertilizer for the coming year. In other words,
this vineyard owner shouldn't have been looking for fruit until year four.
If fruit had grown, he should have let it fall to the ground. Any fruit in
the fourth year was supposed to be an offering, and he could eat of it in
the fifth year. To paraphrase, this guy was saying, "I want what I want,
and if I don't see it, I'm not going to give God what He asks. I'm putting
my measurement of success ahead of God's request for faithfulness and
trust!"

It's not just a coincidence that Jesus's ministry, which spanned three and a half years, produced no reliable fruit for the first three years. The disciples were unreliable and untrustworthy; they came and went, some left, and even those who stayed didn't really get it. They fought among themselves for status; they argued, connived, and betrayed. They promised to stand by Jesus at all times, and when the trial came, they denied even knowing who He was. At the crucifixion, all Jesus had to show for His efforts was one denier, one betrayer, and ten long-distance runners. The fourth year of His ministry concluded with His own offering of Himself to God, and the fifth year began with the Feast of Pentecost—the first fruits of the harvest.

It's no wonder that Jesus told the followers, as He entered the city of Jerusalem on His way to the Passover, that unless a seed falls to the ground, it abides alone. But if it falls to the ground, it brings forth much fruit. Not even Jesus would make a judgment about success or failure prior to the fifth year!

The five-year pattern shows up in so many endeavors, and it seems that there's no way around it. We use the five-year benchmark to evaluate the likelihood of a new business succeeding. We tell entrepreneurs not to expect income for three years from a new startup, and we look to year five for viability. If we plant a new product or service, we don't look for profit for three years, and invest everything back into it. What if we expected this, and used any fruit from year four to benefit our community? What if we used the five-year expectation as a plan for organic growth, rather than thinking that *we* are the ones to beat the pattern in our ministries? And what if I came back to my pastor in year three of a new program or ministry endeavor, and offered to dig around and throw more manure at it for year four?

Growing versus Building

Jesus seldom used metaphors of building in His parables, and the few times that He does, they're often warnings. "Whoever starts out to build a building without counting the cost is unwise" (Luke 14:28 paraphrase).

Most often He used metaphors of growth and nature to illustrate the kingdom. "The kingdom of heaven is like a seed" (Mark 4:31) and the spirit is like water, "springing up into eternal life" (John 4:14). Most of His parables were about farming and growth, not the sudden act of building. Building takes human planning and control, and is according to our timetables. Sowing seed is about living in the rhythm of the seasons, where there is no control. Like the sower, who sows without thinking about where the seed is landing and has no clue how it grows, we are sowing seed wherever we go.

I know this argues against the current trend of "intentionality," which is a kind of claiming control and responsibility. Instead of drinking coffee with a friend, I'm intentionally trying to change them or bring about what I envision. But sowing and reaping are very different; the seed will grow as long as there's rain and sun, and both are beyond my control. The Creation account puts it like this:

> Let the earth bring forth grass, the herb yielding seed, *and* the fruit tree yielding fruit after his kind, whose seed *is* in itself, upon the earth: and it was so. And the earth brought forth grass, *and* herb yielding seed after his kind, and the tree yielding fruit, whose seed *was* in itself, after his kind: and God saw that *it was* good. (Genesis 1:11–12)

The earth brings forth grass, herb, and fruit, with seed already in itself; the seed is of its own kind and produces more fruit as it falls to the ground and grows. We don't cause the seed to sprout, since the seed already contains the potential for life and sprouts regardless of our intentions or hopes. Once the seed falls to the ground, by means of birds, animals, or simply gravity, the seed sprouts, and we can water it, but growth comes from the natural created by God. If conditions aren't right, the seed can lie dormant for years until enough moisture and sunlight cause it to sprout. The seed, no matter how old, will always carry within itself the potential for life beyond human volition.

When Adam and Eve are created, they're given the task of keeping the garden. This is more than just tending carrots in rows or pulling a few weeds from a window box. If you've ever lived in a home built in the country, you know how constant the battle is to keep your yard from being reclaimed by nature. Keeping a yard is a never-ending battle with the tenacious weeds and other things that always seem to encroach on the margins of our perfectly manicured yard. And nature is relentless in the battle!

We have a maple tree in our yard, and every spring I battle with seeds that sprout from the previous summer. We need to clean small tree sprouts out of our rain gutters, out of our rock garden, and out of the cracks between sections of sidewalk. It's a constant job of preventing nature from reclaiming what humans have ordered. I've even removed saplings from leftover grass clippings on top of my lawnmower from the last time I mowed in the fall! Tending a yard or a garden is much more about pruning than it is planting, removing what you don't want because it interferes, and preserving what you want to grow. But even if you don't remove and prune, what grows is a result of the relentlessness of the natural order. Our straight lines become overgrown curves within days if we don't stay vigilant, and God calls this good.

We seldom hear metaphors of growth when church is the topic. We sing about building the kingdom, go to growth conferences where strategies of building are discussed, and hear constant reminders about how we need to build the kingdom. The title might be "growth," but the thinking is "building." But here's the difference. Growth is about a natural process that God created and controls, while building is about what we do to plan, change, and control. Building is about imposing our will on our terms on our timetable.

In the upper Midwest, we have a very distinct construction season, but that doesn't mean we don't build buildings in the wintertime. The cost of the technology, equipment, and machinery is much higher, and usually more than the value of waiting three months, so some things are scheduled around the seasonal interruptions of cold and snow. Growth, on the other hand, connects us to the rhythm of the seasons.

Thinkers from Henry David Thoreau to contemporary media critics have lamented the modern world's disconnection from nature that results from technology. When we lose our connection to nature, we lose an important part of our connection to God. We begin to think of nature as something to be avoided, hurried through, controlled, eliminated, or even idolized. We sell cars by showing the viewer a four-wheel-drive that can conquer the highest peak—a peak that none of the buyers would ever consider driving on. The only times we show or consider nature is when we want to fix it, overcome it, or avoid it. This isn't to say that we succeed, but that nostalgia for Eden is one of the most powerful selling tools in advertising's arsenal, but even then, the vision is distorted by lack of familiarity and by distance.

My grandfather farmed and taught school in the early part of the twentieth century, when agriculture was undergoing the shift from horsepower to steam, and then to gasoline. The degree of trust in the natural order is truly amazing; he was fond of observing that there are no atheists in foxholes or farm fields. The farmer had to put nearly every spare penny into seed, and after planting, had to wait for the seasons to see if it grew or not. If the weather was bad, so were their fortunes; if the weather was good, the abundance they enjoyed was experienced by everyone else, and the value of their surplus went down.

Every spring was a gamble, and every summer like a slow slot machine, where each of the dials took a month to snap into position. Every autumn was like watching what dropped into the cup at the bottom of the machine, where what dropped into your cup could only be valued after seeing what dropped into your neighbor's cup. I once asked Grandpa if he ever gambled, and he said he didn't need to. He farmed.

Modern farming allows us to grow much larger and more efficient crops, which is another way of saying that we've learned to eliminate many of the vagaries. We can even grow food in vertical farms, indoors, and using artificial light, constant monitoring for nutrients and water, and constant temperatures. We can genetically manipulate the properties of seeds, making them more resistant to parasites and blights, but in spite of all of the technology, we've never been able to create life. We still depend on the life that is in the seed, and still need to be faithful to believe that if we plant and water, the seed will grow. But we're still using a natural process of growth, which we can't create or copy, only manipulate.

Building is much easier to talk about because we're mostly guys doing the teaching, and we can envision the shape and size; draw it up into charts and graphs; break it into steps, assuming linear and exponential returns; draw up material lists and statistics; and set timetables. We can squeeze out inefficiencies in costs and processes. I'm not saying that women can't or don't do this; just that it's easier for men to think like this for one simple fact: we can't bring forth life! We can't grow anything except bigger stomachs and hair in our ears. We have so little connection to the natural order of growth that we can't do much more than create spreadsheets to show when to water, fertilize, and cut our lawns. Building is external to us, while growth requires acceptance of much beyond our control.

We gravitate toward metaphors of building because of the element of control. Building is about bending nature to our will and measuring the outcome. I succeed as a builder if I control more, and it's much easier to do that than it is to trust my fortune to the weather. I've spent quite a bit of time in and around commercial construction, and I've learned that success and profit come not from working harder, but from finding new or better materials or processes that save time in the field.

Like the loaf of bread at the convenience store, we don't make money doing what everyone wants or expects; we make it by doing the unplanned, essential parts that were overlooked by the designers and architects. The bread just pays for itself, but it's the donuts and pastries that make money. One local convenience store chain is now selling dinner kits, and their commercial features a busy husband cooking dinner for his wife after a long day at work. The convenience store clerk suggests the dinner kit; the man buys it, boils or microwaves it, then serves it with two candles and a bottle of wine. Solving the overlooked planning for the busy family is the need, the dinner kit is the solution, and the payoff is the implied dessert that hubby can count on later on.

Metaphors of building become awkward when we apply them to natural processes, and even more so when we try to think of spiritual processes. My son, who is twenty-one towers over his parents, but not because we designed him that way. It's a combination of genetics and nutrition, and we didn't have much to do with either. We may say, "That's what happens if you keep feeding them," but we wouldn't say, "We thought he'd look good if we designed and built a third story." We would talk about raising children, not building them.

We might talk about building character, but think of how much different it feels if we think about God growing His character in us, compared to us building character in our children. It feels awkward to think about building kindness and compassion. How would we do that? By digging holes, pouring in concrete, welding steel, and pounding nails? And if I say I want to build a friendship, what pops into your thoughts? All of the processes and steps I need to take to produce a desired relationship, to take it to the next level. How do I define, control, and measure the outcomes against design? And how much different is it to think that I'm building it, or that God is growing it? Notice how the element of control disappears, and I'm left trusting?

Consider some other ways that building differs from growing:

1. "The seed is of its own kind." Oak trees produce seeds that grow into oak trees, and pines become pines. Potatoes grow into potatoes, not penguins. We can manipulate some of the properties of the seeds through genetic engineering, make them more resistant to parasites or eliminate characteristics we don't want, but they still produce the kind of growth that God has designed. No matter how much I wish that my radishes would become redwoods, it just isn't going to happen because I want it to. Or because I can create a spreadsheet.

2. The species and size that the plant will grow to is determined by the plant's DNA. Its maximum size is already imprinted at the moment the seed sprouts. I can enhance the final size with careful nutrition, but the size of the plant at maturity will still fall within the range for that plant. That isn't up to me.

3. Any effort to grow the plant beyond its normal size will be unstable. If you've ever tried to do body sculpting by exercising or dieting, you'll know that attaining your goal is only one step; maintaining your ideal weight or muscle development takes constant work and vigilance. And the older you get, the harder it is to maintain the goal. It's a matter of diminishing returns. Again, we can enhance natural processes, but we don't create them or take them beyond the range of what's possible. If you have one body type, you can build muscle around it, but you won't change the basic shape.

4. Each plant has its own life cycle, and each plant grows at its own pace. It also withers and dies at its own pace. The plant will grow to its maturity, produce its seeds, repeat its cycle, and grow old and die on its own timetable. Its point of ending is written in its beginning. We can extend it within its range, but not beyond it.

Imagine hearing this at the next church growth seminar: "When you go into the city to plant a church body, don't count on any growth for at least a year or two. Anything that grows in the first three years will probably be unstable, and we shouldn't expect it to be stable. Let it fall to the ground. Anything that grows in year four will be an offering to the Lord. Look for ways to send those people to bless another ministry. Plant them elsewhere! If nothing happens in year four, then go find another field. Now let's eat cake!"

Over the long term, understand that what you plant won't grow beyond a size that God's already purposed. It has a life cycle that is already determined at its inception. And any effort to push it beyond its natural size and lifespan will be unstable. Don't set any goals or expectations beyond what God shows you. And remember that Jesus told us that the world is the field, not the church; the church is the barn. So don't think that success lies in planning a succession of bigger barns, and don't think, *I need to tear down my barn and build a bigger one because my harvest is great.*

Organizational development experts find that there are natural growth points in any organization, and growing beyond a breakpoint takes more resources and efforts directed to maintaining than to growth. There's even a name for the size where you have to direct most of your resources to convincing members that you're still small and intimate. It's called Dunbar's Number. That number...wait for it...is around 150. In other words, once you hit 150, you'll spend most of your energy convincing people that you're still smaller than 150! Isn't it amazing that most churches in the U.S. have around 125 members, and few go beyond 200?

I've been part of ministry teams that struggled to break 200, only to see them revert back to around 165 every single time. The senior pastor tried every new growth strategy that came along, from big blue buses to small groups. And every time the church grew past 200, it would slowly revert. The pastor struggled with feelings of failure, but in essence, he was struggling against God's design for that church.

And the pressure that was put on volunteer leadership and faithful members was enormous. Many of them burned out over the constant pressure to produce bigger outcomes. Over thirty years and two pastoral changes, that church's attendance is still the same. They've built a new building, created a website, established small groups, gone to virtual meetings, developed a killer worship team, advertised on Christian radio, and worn cool T-shirts, but they've never gone sustainably past Dunbar's Number.

We don't control any of the things that mark the effort as a success. Our job is to be faithful—to sow on every field, wait patiently, and let God bring forth what He has purposed to grow. Spiritual life is much like natural life; we don't create it ourselves.

When Theresa and I were planning a family, we weren't able to become pregnant for ten years. People would assume that we were just young and self-centered, and that in time, we'd come around. Some even prayed that we'd grow in maturity to the point where we could look beyond ourselves, while we were sitting in front of them. One of them later apologized to Theresa, saying that it never occurred to her that we might be trying with no results.

In time, we accepted the possibility that we might be unable to conceive, and we began looking into the adoption process. That was interrupted by my return to college and moving halfway across the country to establish a campus ministry. And God, who has a great sense of humor, confirmed our obedience by bringing our oldest daughter into the world one year to the day after we moved to Pennsylvania.

In the last chapter, we talked about circular time rather than linear time, and how oral cultures live in the circle of time, with the future behind them and the past kept alive and fresh in front of them. We talked about how linear time leads us to judge our past by putting periods instead of commas on experience, in order to judge whether they are worth keeping. We talked about how the beginnings and endings we place on experiences distort them, causing us to reject the very things He has done in order to try to game God into a future we think we want but that He'll never do. Finally, we heard about how this puts us in the place of discontent, as if we're crucified between two thieves, stealing our joy and peace.

In this chapter, we've listened to how oral cultures would think about success or failure. We've listened to how the notion of success is based on the assumption that all human activity can be measured by profit and loss, and how we learned to put standards of judgment on experience based on profit in order to deem them a success. Oral cultures put the emphasis on faithfulness, which we hear Jesus do over and over: "Well done, good and faithful servant" (Matthew 25:23).

We've looked at the parable of the sower as more than just a story about soil quality and yields versus investment, but as a story about how little knowledge or skill the sower needed to be faithful. And we've heard about how the metaphor of sowing and growth can be a challenge to our notions of success, establishing an enormous amount of uncertainty. In fact, the only two things that the sower is certain about is that there's seed in the bag and that the master has told him to sow. Seasons, times, and yields are all the Master's responsibility and to the Master's glory.

Tension Between Two Worlds: Faithfulness vs. Success

1. What scriptural examples can you find that demonstrate faithfulness but that were not successful?

2. Can you think of a time when you were faithful but unsuccessful? How did you reconcile the two conflicting sets of standards?

3. Can you judge something as a success or failure without imposing time limits on the outcomes? How does time relate to the purposes of One who stands outside of time?

4. If success depends on comparison of ourselves to others or comparison of ourselves to our expectations, how can we lead from a perspective of faithfulness only?

5. How would the notion of faithfulness affect your church planning? Your assessment of ministry effectiveness?

6. How would using metaphors of planting and harvesting rather than planning and building affect your teaching? Your leadership? How you teach others to lead?

7. How would the five-year pattern of planting and sowing affect your thinking and teaching?

8. How would our faith community be different if we taught faithfulness to God and to each other only?

5

I Have Called You Friends

I was listening to the local Christian station today as I drove, and I heard an expert on Christian living say, "God doesn't want your money. He wants to have a relationship with you." We've heard it often—in teaching and preaching, in our songs, in the altar calls, in all the books that line the shelves of the physical and online Christian bookstore. Being the inquisitive sort, I always want to ask, "But what relationship does He want?"

That's an important question, because by definition, I already have one. By definition, I have a relationship with every person I pass on the road. To most, I'm a stranger. To some, like the lady in the gray Buick who is always late for work and needs to pass me on a narrow road so she can save ten seconds, I'm an obstacle. I wonder if her job description says "must be willing to risk your life and the lives of everyone else on the road to sell these widgets." She's my reason to leave the house exactly by 6:57 a.m.

By definition, I have a relationship with you, my reader. We've probably never met, but I hope that someday we will. By definition, I have a relationship with every other person on the face of the earth. My relationship with God might be as a stranger, it might be as a rebellious son, it might be as a scoffing challenger, it might be as an aloof and distant student of His works or words, or it might be as someone who has been transformed from death to life and adopted into His family. I always and already have a relationship with God, since He made me, so asking what kind of relationship is critical.

I'd go so far as to suggest that all Christian books, literature, songs, sermons, and teachings are about our relationship with God and with each other. My local radio station has experts on every hour (I know they're experts, because the sound engineers add echo to the announcer's voice when she says the word *expert*. Kind of like an aural version of a ransom note.) We definitely have a certain type of relationship in mind when we use the word, and we always teach to that word. We just don't bother to define what we mean most of the time, since the word has become so common. We assume that everyone knows what we mean. We all know what a relationship is, right?

What if what we think of as the ultimate and desired relationship isn't what Jesus invited His followers to enter? In His parables, Jesus called us sons, daughters, children, sheep, wheat, servants, and trees. He spoke of mustard seeds, pearls, and fish. Every single one of His parables had a relationship embedded in it. Sons and daughters had certain obligations and privileges; second sons had different privileges than the firstborn. But what was the highest and best relationship He invited His followers to enter? In other words, what would His hearers have heard when He spoke?

I believe that one of the most incredible statements uttered by Jesus is when He said, "I have called you friends" (John 15:15). It's one of those statements that we gloss over without thinking about it, since *friend* is such a commonly used term. We all know what *friend* means, right? Since Facebook, which redefined what a friend is, we've all understood that Jesus wants to see more pictures of our cats.

The word *friend* has changed meaning several times over the last two thousand years, and while it would be fun to trace the lineage of the word, it's more helpful for us to look at how we think of *friend* today, how we thought of *friend* in the recent past, and how Jesus' listeners may have understood the word as it was used in biblical times by oral thinkers. Suffice it to say that the issue of friendship was of great concern to early writers. Aristotle addressed friendship at great length in the *Ethics*, Cicero wrote an entire book devoted to exploring the meaning of friendship in Roman culture at the end of the first century CE, and the book of Proverbs is full of aphorisms about friendship.

I'll go out on a limb here and suggest that while there were many things Jesus said that offended the leaders of His community, not many of them warranted His execution. Even some of those that we think would have caused Him to be stoned wouldn't have. For instance, the claim to be the Messiah may have been extreme, but one of the reasons it probably wouldn't have been enough to warrant His execution is that the claim wasn't all that unusual.

When the religious leaders discussed what to do about Jesus, they cited a number of examples when people had made the same claim, and how they had ended up. The suggestion to leave Him alone and see what came of Him was born out of several examples of people who had made the claim in the past. They'd all ended up dead and their followers scattered, without the leaders taking action. They had a history of dealing with the claim, which seemed to be defended by God Himself through circumstance. Laws are not created to prevent people from doing something they aren't already doing! And the fact that the leaders can cite examples, and that they have a history of dealing with the claim, suggests that the claim wasn't something new. Jesus wasn't the first, and His followers clearly weren't the first people, to claim that He was the One.

It's obvious that the meaning of the word *friend* has changed over time, but what I want us to understand is that there was something very threatening about how Jesus made the statement. His listeners would have heard something far more audacious than a claim to be the Messiah. I want us to realize that friendship in an oral culture is very different than it is in a literate twenty-first-century culture. I want us to understand that the highest relationship among Jesus' followers was friendship, as they understood it, and it's that relationship that Jesus offers to us. I also want to show that we have multiple understandings of friendship, but that what our heart tells us is different from what our heads are taught. In short, while we might describe friendship in modern terms, our hearts understand and yearn for friendship as oral thinkers.

In order to tune our ear to what Jesus' hearers might have heard, let's get a clear understanding of modern friendship. In order to do that, we need to talk briefly about models, metaphors, and theory. The term *theory* was introduced by Greek thinkers, and I like the way it works. It meant "a way of seeing."

A theory was an explanation of something, using models, examples, reasoning, and metaphors. Since the advent of the scientific method, we've redefined theory to be similar to a hypothesis—a statement of relationships of cause and effect between something observed and an outcome. Hypotheses are tested through controlled experimentation, and once duplicated to the point of confidence, they are elevated to theory. Theories are further tested, and eventually take on the status of laws. For example, we refer to gravity as a law instead of a theory. We may find out more about how gravity functions as our ability to test and model becomes more sophisticated.

When non-scientists use the term *theory*, we usually mean a simple explanation of cause and effect. These can be subject to all sorts of distortions. For instance, we have a smoke detector in our kitchen that's placed close to our stove. When we cook something at more than 400 degrees, like a pizza, the extra heat rising to the ceiling causes the smoke detector to go off. When that happens, we open the window over the kitchen sink to bring in more fresh air. One of our two indoor cats loves to sit in open windows and smell the outside air. After a few months with us, she's learned that when the smoke alarm goes off, the window gets opened. Now, anytime we start preheating the oven, she jumps onto the windowsill and stares at us.

Our theory is the cat has learned by repetition that when the smoke alarm rings, we open the window, so that is her signal to come running. She's been conditioned to the point that she associates the window with the oven anytime we turn the oven on.

While that's a plausible explanation, it could also be wrong. She may hate the smell of pepperoni and be seeking fresh air. We could test our observations by holding a lighted candle up to the smoke alarm without turning on the oven, and see if she acts the same way. We could turn the oven on low, so that there isn't enough heat to trigger the alarm, and see if it's the oven opening that triggers her response. In time, with enough repetitions and changing of variables, we can discover the connection between one variable and another, and generalize to more than just a guess. However, the fact that our theory may be wrong doesn't mean much; the behavior still goes on, we laugh about it, and we eat our pizza. One theory is as good as another, as both explain her behavior. In other words, a theory can be incorrect, but it's still functional and can guide our decisions to our benefit.

For example, one area that's been studied in many disciplines is how to make decisions in groups. Many models of decision-making have been discovered and described over the years, from Dewey's reflexive method, to SWOT analysis, to SWAG analysis. We regularly see some new method or model of decision-making in the latest book on management or leadership. But the meta study of leadership methods shows that which method a group uses is less important than the fact that they're using any one of them.

Some decision-making methodologies work better for one type of problem than another, and there's often a misfit between decision-making methods and the task to be carried out. But the bottom line is that groups that choose and follow a decision-making model tend, over time, to make better decisions, and to make them faster. They also tend to have better buy-in from members, and to have higher satisfaction than groups that don't use a decision-making method. In short, any method is better than no method. It's not the method; it's the fact that the group has become cohesive by sharing a set of rules and procedures about how they'll do their business.*

When I taught small-group communication and decision-making, I'd use a quiz at the end of the section on decision-making that would both test and illustrate this. Students had been working on projects regularly in small groups both inside and outside of class, and the quiz was taken in their regular groups. They were given three extremely vague questions about some element of group theory, and asked to select a question and craft a single response on paper for the group. They needed to choose a question, define what the question meant to them, answer it using a theory and an example, and get it written down on a single sheet of paper in twenty-five minutes. The only way that a group could do this was if they had been using a decision-making discipline in their out-of-class work times. The test didn't measure their knowledge; it measured if they'd learned to use a decision-making method without being told to do so.

At the end of the twenty-five minutes, the groups turned in their answers. Their paper would either be blank and they'd be frustrated, or there would be a paragraph or two outlining a response. Any written response required at least three to five decisions along the way. Any response would be acceptable, and would demonstrate that they were actually applying content from the course in their own group work. Someone would occasionally object that it wasn't fair, since I didn't tell them what was really being tested, but tests can be about knowledge as well as whether skills are applied, and the group work they had done to this point without observation could easily have been done by one responsible group member while the rest sat by. The

* Hirowkawa, R.Y. (1983). Group Communication and Problem Solving Effectiveness; An investigation of group phases. Human Communication Research, 9, 291-305.

point was that using any method was better than no method, even if it wasn't the best method.

When it comes to teaching about relationships, an incorrect theory of behavior may be better than no theory at all. Modern theory still works, but it produces something less than it could if other theories were used. And it's here that we circle back to the idea of friendship. Our modern theory of friendship is extremely different from what a first-century oral thinker would have carried around in their heads. We can still use our modern theories of friendship, and the explanations may work for us today, but they aren't at all what a first-century hearer would have understood.

Most of our modern Christian teaching about friendship follows one particular model, put forth in the 1960s. Even if the writers don't know it, the terminology they use, and that has become so familiar as to be unquestioned, is taken from this model. Before we delve into an oral understanding of friendship, let's spend a few minutes looking at this model and its drawbacks. Along the way, we'll have to look at a second model that's embedded in the first model. That is the notion of how people communicate.

Over the history of thinking about communication, there have been many models that describe how communication works. In fact, every philosopher must first define the tools that are used to think about and arrive at truth, and those tools are words. Every philosopher has to define how words work, what their power is, whether they can be trusted, and whether they even contain or describe truth.

Think back to the Socratic dialogues you were forced to read in history, English, or philosophy courses and how dull they were. One of those you probably had to read was called the *Phaedrus*. It was a dialogue between Socrates and a student, on the danger posed by itinerant teachers of speech who couldn't guarantee that what they were teaching wouldn't lead to error. Socrates called these teachers Sophists. The Sophists taught about how to convince others that something was true, but the danger, according to Socrates, was that persuasion would produce a belief in the truth, but not the truth.

If I teach you to make a chair, the end result is a chair. If I teach you to bake a cake, the outcome is a cake. If I teach you to paint a picture, the outcome is a picture. But if I teach you how to persuade, using words, it ends up in a *belief* that something is true, but it isn't the truth. Thus, it's not a skill; it's an art that should only be entrusted to those who know the truth, and can teach the truth, and are willing to risk their lives to stand for the truth. These are the philosophers, as opposed to the rhetoricians.

The Sophists were a clever bunch. One even argued something like this: 1) There is no such thing as truth. 2) If there was, we couldn't know it since we're human. 3) Even if there was truth and we could know it, we couldn't teach it in our limited language. 4) That's the truth!

In another example, one of the teachers of rhetoric sued a student for not paying his tuition at the end of his course. The teacher argued that if he could convince the judge that he'd taught the student and the student had refused to pay, the teacher should win the case. If the student could convince the judge that he'd learned nothing, it was because he'd become a skilled speaker, which was because of what he'd learned. So, if the teacher convinced the judge, he'd win; if the student convinced the judge that he hadn't learned anything, the teacher would win.

The student countered that he'd learned nothing, and if he could convince the judge, he shouldn't have to pay. If he couldn't convince the judge, it was because he hadn't learned anything, and thus, if he lost, he should win. You can hear the playfulness that reverberates through these examples—a playfulness that shows up in both Jesus' teaching and, every once in a while, Paul's letters.

Shannon-Weaver Model of Communication

The model of communication that permeates all of our current teaching about relationships was first published in 1949 by communication theorist Warren Weaver. He based his theory on a 1949 book by Claude Shannon, *A Mathematical Theory of Communication*. Shannon was an electrical engineer, and his theory was about improving the accuracy of message transmission in telephones and radio. He is regarded as the originator of signal compression, which is used today to reduce electronic messages to their essential elements, and to reproduce them at the other end without distortion. The goal of Shannon's theory was to eliminate uncertainty, reduce ambiguity, and enhance signal fidelity—in short, how to reproduce the message at the other end, without distortion, so that only the original message got through with no signal degradation.

The year 1949 was a time when communication studies were at a crossroads. The classical model of rhetoric, which shared much of its history, theory, and content with English and philosophy departments, was hard-pressed to justify its separate existence.

At the risk of oversimplifying, there was a tremendous amount of government research money available at the end of World War II for any field that could help explain, and hopefully prevent, the kind of atrocities that were only then being uncovered. Sociology, psychology, and what we now know as the social sciences promised research agendas into individual and social behaviors by developing their own theories of social behavior. Communication studies was then a fledgling field, and the model offered by Shannon to address signal degradation in army field telephones looked like a way to ground communication in the hard sciences rather than literary criticism or aesthetics.

At the same time, academic disciplines that could identify, select, and enhance leadership qualities had a tremendous appeal for military research dollars. The field of management studies was the answer, and the theory of communication that came out of hard science (which, to be blunt, had just made the world safe for democracy) was attractive and useful.

In 1949, Weaver republished Shannon's theory under the title *The Mathematical Theory of Communication*, along with a twenty-eight-page introduction, which applied some of Shannon's terminology and concepts to human conversation. The theory was limited in that it had no recognition of context (Shannon was working with telephones and wires), and context wasn't important to the movement of electrons. Subsequent work by other communication theorists supplied some of the missing elements, and added other details to account for the messiness of human activity described through a mathematical model.

Over the next few decades, the Shannon model was applied to the way people talked in any situation or circumstance. Shannon's model has supplied the vocabulary for describing communication in relationships of any kind since its proliferation across the social sciences. The model is still used in basic course textbooks in many disciplines, and the vocabulary of the model is still the default language through which we describe modern-day events. In spite of its ubiquity, the Shannon-Weaver model is really a model of information transmission, where information is a measure of uncertainty or ambiguity. The goal in this approach is to reduce or eliminate uncertainty, not convey meaning.

Shannon's model used highly technical terms to measure and describe elements, like "information entropy" to describe uncertainty in a message. When Weaver and others applied it to human communication, specialized terms were dropped and more accessible terminology was used.

In Shannon's model, Communication begins with a Sender, who wishes to convey some sort of Message to a Receiver. The Sender Encodes the message, selects a Channel to send it to the Receiver, and conveys the Message across the Channel to the Receiver. The Receiver must then Decode the Message back into a thought. If the meaning in the mind of the Sender is the same as the Message in the mind of the Receiver at the end, effective Communication has occurred.*

---

*   Information theory is discussed in Stephen W. Littlejohn: Theories of human communication, Third Edition, Wadsworth publishing, 1989: 42-51.

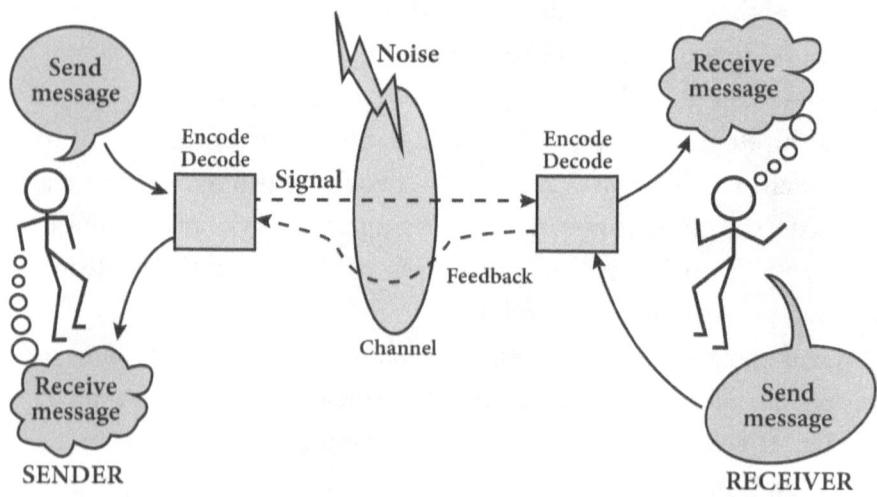

Applied to electronic exchanges, this made sense. Encoding could actually be a code, whether Morse code, voice signal, or some other specialized code meant to prevent others from intercepting it. Channel also made sense, when dealing with electronic frequencies. When applied to speech, one could choose interpersonal, small group, large audience, or mediated by technology. But what seems like a clear-cut distinction becomes vague when the number of participants determines what constitutes a channel. We may speak differently when it's ten people listening to us instead of one person, but calling the difference a channel is a stretch.

Shannon was working at a time when radio was dominant; telegraph had faded but could still be used, and television was in its infancy. Radio could be either wired into a network or short wave. So there actually were channel differences that had to be considered, and choice of channel did much to determine the kinds of degradation a message could encounter.

Later communication theorists introduced missing elements like context, distortion, and feedback, which occur when the receiver becomes the sender and sends a message confirming that the message is what they wanted to get across.

If all of this sounds familiar, it should. It's a description of two-way radio. Shannon illustrates one interesting feature of defining communication. All of our models for human communication are really descriptions of the most up-to-date communication technology. He created his model to address radio and telephone, and therefore had no awareness of anything visual. Messages could only go one way at a time, and speakers took turns sending and receiving. Interference came from resistance in the wires and degradation of the signal through switching, and the surrounding environment wasn't considered at all. Finally, Shannon had no interest in meaning, only accuracy. Shannon later observed, when asked about message content, that "sometimes the messages have meaning." But his concern wasn't about meaning; it was about accurately delivering the message at the other end.

In a nutshell, Shannon describes a situation where the speaker's intent governs the success or failure of the interaction. If *my* message gets to you, it's good; if you get something that's not exactly the same, it's a failure. This works very well in a relationship of asymmetrical power, where accuracy and message fidelity are key. For instance, when I go through the drive-thru at my local burger joint, and I yell my order into the hippo's mouth, accuracy is very important. I want exactly what I ordered, nothing more and nothing less. If I'm a surgeon operating on a patient, and I give an order to an assistant, I want the nurse to do exactly what I've requested. The consequences may be more or less important than the burger example, but it's still *my* intent that governs. In other words, it's not important that *we* understand each other; it's important that *you* think like I do at the end.

Besides reinforcing a power difference, there are other gaps in the Shannon Weaver model. Our experience tells us that much of the message we send (using the model's terminology) comes through what we think of as non-verbal means. Tone, cadence, pacing of words, and inflection all have a lot to do with the meaning we are trying to convey. Likewise, gestures, posture, facial expression, and other physical elements can emphasize, describe, model, and even negate what we've just said. We also know that people don't take turns as regularly as the model would suggest.

When we're conversing, the attention I give you has a lot to do with how you say it, and my physical gestures or expressions affect what you're saying. Frowning, crossing my arms, fidgeting, or turning slightly away suggest that I disagree before you even complete your thought. Smiling, nodding, and standing closer to you suggest that I agree, and you may increase your pace or raise the tone of your voice for emphasis. I may even talk at the same time as you, and in Weaver's simple model, that's a failure.

You can clearly see how the model fails to describe the subtle ways that we interact as humans. How would we describe poetry, which isn't necessarily about recreating my thought in your mind, but often seeks to evoke an experience? How would we describe song lyrics, which are frequently about evoking an emotion? How would we describe the stuff we do that isn't about getting you to think like me—the stuff at the beginning and ending of a sermon, for instance? Theorists use the term *phatic* communication to describe the parts of our talking that are about the social and emotional dimensions of our relationship.

We even go *meta*, which is when we talk about the meaning of the way we're interacting ("Don't look at me like that when I'm talking!"). The popular term for this is "small talk," which points to another important limitation: the model is gendered. It led theorists of the 1950s and 1960s to assume that men and women talk differently, and women are more likely to pay attention to the social and emotional elements, which were relegated to "small" things in the world of theory. But that's not true at all. Men and women both talk about emotions, but some are more likely to tell a story or quote a movie line that *demonstrates* the emotion rather than *naming* the emotion.

There are many examples in our daily experience where replication of my idea in your mind is the last thing I want to consider. What is the message of a eulogy? What idea do you want to recreate in the minds of the hearers at a wedding? How important is what the speaker says at a high school graduation? Does every utterance send a message? How about silence? It's meaningful, but is silence a message? These are examples that, because they don't fit the model very well, don't get considered. But they're an important part of our existence.

Even though later theorists moved beyond the simplicity of the model, the basic thinking of the model, as well as the terminology of the model, persist in virtually every textbook in every discipline. Through the 1970s and 1980s, Shannon's terms became the default language through which we described relationships and interactions of any kind. Most popular books on management, business success, leadership, and relationships still use the terms of the Shannon model to describe their subject. We send messages through channels, we describe failure as a "breakdown," and we talk about "sending messages."

Sometimes this can be absurd. I remember the moment I heard a reporter ask a question during a press conference. It was during the first Desert Storm, and a general was describing the number of military sorties that had been flown the previous day. He described the hundreds of flights, the tons of ordnance that had been dropped, the number of targets that had been destroyed or bombed, and the number of casualties. "General," said the reporter, "you've dropped X number of bombs, X tons of ordnance, etc. Are you trying to send Saddam Hussein a message?" The look on the general's face was priceless, as he patiently tried to explain that no, we weren't trying to send a message, we were trying to eradicate his genetic line.

It's become a staple of political talk to read disagreement as sending a message of opposition to our own position, and then imputing bad intent about that person's character. In these days of COVID, we've all heard that opposing shutdowns is sending the message that we hate Grandma. We aren't willing to consider that a refusal to order everyone to wear a mask might be because we aren't sure that such an order would fit within the constitutional framework of federal or state authority.

Who has the authority when we're talking about wearing a garment to cover a portion of our bodies?

My state health department can tell me to wear pants in a restaurant for health reasons. My state's civil code can tell me to wear pants in public to protect the innocence of children who occasionally go without pants, and to prevent people who walk down the street from being traumatized. OSHA can tell me to wear pants when I'm welding at my place of employment. OSHA can also tell me to wear a mask when I'm in a hazardous environment in my workplace, and they can define what kind of mask is needed for the hazard. OSHA can fine my employer for not providing the training and the masks, and for not enforcing the rule to wear them.

But asking who would have the authority to issue an order to wear a piece of medical or workplace safety at all times outside of my home is a tougher call. And asking who could do it, how they could do it, and how it would be enforced are legal and procedural questions, not a revelation of my hatred for an earlier generation. Michael Lewis' 2021 book "The Premonition" explores how no one had a clear understanding of what a public health official's roles and powers were, let alone the general public. That includes the White House, the media, and the Center for Disease Control.

At the same time, I understand that your wish to protect yourself and your loved ones from a life-threatening virus while going about your life is a valid concern. I understand that you want to do everything you can to be safe, and that you're willing to go the extra mile rather than fall a foot short. I understand that you don't want to run my life, limit my freedom, or make me look stupid. During emergencies, we allow for all sorts of intrusions on personal liberties, so asking for someone to tell you what to do and doing it doesn't mean you're a bad person.

I may choose to wear a mask for my and my family's protection, while disagreeing with the idea that a governor can decree mask wearing under emergency powers. I may question whether a president can call the fight against the virus a "war" and then issue orders that might override what a state would have as a mechanism for such an order. I may even, in a moment of trolling, ask how we could say a leader failed to *make* us wear masks by ordering us to wear them, when we've made it our life mission to resist anything that leader has said.

None of those questions make you a bad person, but mask wearing has been reduced in public talk to sending a message that you're a bad person who hates other people. Finally, as a senior citizen, I wonder why we don't question if you hate Grandpa? He's never part of the discussion! All of this illustrates the extent to which we've internalized the notion that everything is a message, and that I can discern your intent in that message.

Models are helpful in describing and understanding complex things, but they are also risky in that they show us certain things that fit the model. They also cause us to look away from things that don't fit the model. And finally, they cause us to think of what's being described only in the terms of the model. One of the best examples of this is "breakdown" of communication. By modeling communication as a mechanical process, it's easy to describe failure as a breakdown. But machines break down; processes don't. Most of our misunderstandings come because we bypass each other, not because something breaks down.

Later models added some of the missing elements back in, but as secondary features. They still retain the basic elements: a focus on the words; beginning and ending with the speaker's intent; privileging idea replication over meaning; modeling as a mechanical process; and preserving distance, turn taking, and asymmetrical power. And notice that it begins and ends with the speaker's message; it's about the speaker, not both parties. The focus is on replicating the speaker's thought, making it about the speaker at the expense of the receiver. In other words, our models may be different at the theoretical level, but the models used in most of our teaching material about relationships of any kind retain the same language, concepts, and terminology of the telephone model.

What happens when we apply our understanding of communication as a 1940s telephone exchange to the notion of the Creator speaking to us? How could the disciples have spoken to one another before the invention of the telephone? And if we describe the communication in a marriage in the terms above, would we call that a healthy relationship? Yet this is the model that has become so embedded in our relationship books that it hardly needs to be explained. The terminology of sender, receiver, feedback, sending messages, getting our message across, effectiveness and efficiency, and noise have become the default understanding in our teaching materials.

For example, FranklinCovey is one of the more popular sources of leadership material for pastors and church leaders over the last thirty years. In a 2020 book called *Management Mess to Leadership Success*, Scott Miller describes Steven Covey's take on effective and ethical leadership communication thus:

> Thankfully, Steven R. Covey tackled this philosophical topic in his book *The Speed of Trust*. He characterized talking straight as "honesty in action" expressed as telling the truth and leaving the right impression. He wrote that effective leaders use straight talk that is "tempered by skill, tact, and good judgment."
>
> As leaders, our ability to talk straight comes down to using clear, accurate, and simple language to ensure that what is said is what is heard and, perhaps, most important, that what is being heard is being understood. Leaders who talk straight

- Call things by their right names using common, plain language

- Don't spin or position for the sake of posturing

- Tell the truth in diplomatic yet clear language

- Don't try to sound more intelligent than they are

Leaders who talk straight leave their listeners clear about the intended message because there was nothing added to distract or confuse. No extra slides. No long effusive speeches. No multisyllable words to impress or intimidate. They don't leave room for misinterpretation or guessing. They stay as far from spin as possible.*

All of this is intended to guarantee that only the speaker's intent remains, and only the speaker's thought is conveyed and received. Anything that strays from the speaker's meaning is not only bad, but unethical and dishonest. By this standard, however, anything Jesus taught through story, parable, verse, psalm, or allusion would have been dismissed.

The Rhetorical Situation and Aristotle

If people in Jesus' day wouldn't have thought of communication in mid-twentieth-century terms and values, how would they have described it? The Proverbs are full of comments that display oral thinking about communication. We can't really say that the wisdom sayings *define* communication, since the notion of defining requires a written dictionary that everyone can turn to as an authority. Rather, they describe word use as powerful, creative, and potentially dangerous in the mouth of someone not under discipline.

One modern theorist, Lloyd Bitzer, laid out a modern restatement of a classical approach to speech-making. He started by noting that no one crafts a speech unless a situation happens where speech would be appropriate. Instead of starting with a great idea in the speaker's mind, and trying to recreate it in the hearer's mind, Bitzer suggests that there are some situations that present us with problems that need to be modified,

---

*   Scott Jeffrey Miller, *Management Mess to Leadership Success* (Salt Lake City: Franklin Covey Co., 2020), 112-113.

and only words will solve the problem. The term Bitzer uses is *exigence*, which is an imperfection that is marked by urgency. Not only is there an issue that can only be addressed by saying something, there's a time limit within which something must be said.*

A good example that springs to mind is the things we say at a funeral or visitation. There's obviously a problem; there's been a death, and someone we know is grieving. While a casserole can help, it's the things we say that help bridge the emotional gaps, and there's clearly a time during which we should say something. If we wait too long, what we say isn't as effective, and if we speak too early, it's wasted. No one crafts a eulogy and then goes around looking for a funeral at which to share it. No one practices (unless you're a mortician) the kinds of things we say to comfort one another. Yet we all have a pretty good idea that something needs to be said, and only words will do.

Not all situations that call for speech are bad, however. Graduations and weddings are situations where there's an exigence. Both are moments when things change reality for everyone involved. Both are moments that call for toasts, memories, speeches, and vows. And both are moments where the participants' status changes from that time forth. There are things we say at events like this that just don't work at other times. There are many types of situations like this, where what is spoken changes circumstances: we declare war, we announce an engagement, or we mark a transition by a ceremony that involves speaking.

In addition to an exigence (an imperfection marked by urgency), there's a *rhetorical audience* or hearer. These are the people who have an interest in the outcome of what is said, and can act as a result of what they hear. Not everyone who is present is part of this audience, for not everyone has an interest or can act. If one of your friends passes away and I go to the funeral with you, I'm there for your support. Unless I'm close to the person who died, I'm not emotionally involved the way

---

* Bitzer, Lloyd, "The Rhetorical Situation," Philosophy & Rhetoric 1, no. 1 (January 1968): 3.

you are, and my interest isn't the same. Hearing good things about the deceased won't change my life through closure. I'm present, but I'm not really someone whose imperfection can be cleared up. If you are one of those who have an interest and can act as a result, you are part of the functional audience.

As well, Bitzer suggests that each situation has its own *constraints:* limitations and possibilities that shape what can be said. As long as we stay within those limits, it doesn't matter what we say, as much as it matters that we act within the appropriate time and say the right kinds of things. At the funeral, we all know the kinds of things we're expected to avoid. We know not to be too frank, and we turn the negatives into positive attributes. If the deceased argued with everyone while alive, we say that they really knew how to liven up a dull moment.

There are all sorts of things we can say at a funeral that we wouldn't feel comfortable saying at other times. We're free to express grief, bewilderment, uncertainty, and loss in words we'd never use at a football game. We can tell stories about the person who passed away that exemplify their personality, and we can laugh about those things. Graduations and weddings have their own sets of constraints on what we say. There are things we probably shouldn't say, and there are things that would be appropriate. As long as we say wedding stuff at the wedding, or graduation stuff at the graduation, it's good. It's the emotional needs of the people who are invested in the outcome, and whose needs come to the surface, that are the focus of a spoken response.

If we use Shannon's mathematical model to describe and evaluate communication, we'd have a hard time seeing any of this. We'd evaluate if the speaker chose the right way to encode their message, if they chose the best channel (text, phone call, Zoom, face-to-face.) We'd evaluate whether the speaker overcame the noise in getting their message across the distance, and we'd look at whether the listener was able to arrive at the same understanding as the speaker intended.

Did they provide the kind of feedback that confirms the original speaker's intent? Was there distortion or error in decoding the message back into ideas? And the judgment we'd make is if the communication was good or bad based on whether the message came through. Finally, models go from descriptive, to evaluative, to instructive by describing communication in terms of the model; evaluate using the logic and elements of the model; and then teach how people should communicate better using the terms and logic of the model. What starts out as a description-measuring device becomes the rule.

The classical model is evaluative and prescriptive too, but in an entirely different way. Instead of asking if the speaker was effective at getting their message across, we'd ask if the speaker was sensitive to the situation, recognized their listeners' needs and concerns in the moment, understood what would be the right kind of thing to say in response, and did so with the right timing. But all of these things don't come out of the speaker being clever or having a great idea that needs to be conveyed to the hearer. They come out of the speaker being grounded in a community that has clear understanding of the right kinds of things to do and say.

The good utterance isn't the one that is effective, efficient, or memorable; it's the one that's timely and appropriate to the moment for the listener. The Shannon model puts the speaker at the beginning and end of the moment, while the classical model puts the hearer and the community at the beginning, end, and center of the moment. Shannon is about me getting my way, while Bitzer is about you hearing what *you* need to hear because I've cared. Shannon's model, which is grounded in literacy, says, "It's not important that we understand each other. It's important that you understand me." The classical model, grounded in orality, says, "It's not really important that I say the right thing; it's important that you hear the right kinds of things said that help you."

My son was born when I was forty-five. He's our second unexpected gift; in fact, we named him Ryan Matthew, which means "little king, gift from God." Ryan came into the world on the Monday following the Saturday that my own father passed away. That whole weekend was a blur. I went from the hospital on Saturday afternoon to meeting with the mortician, along with my family, on Sunday afternoon. As we were naming descendants for the obituary, I listed Ryan as a grandson, and it was the first time we revealed his name. We had the gender reveal at the mortician's conference room table. Can you imagine how confused the mortician felt as my family all started congratulating Theresa and me? In twenty-five years in the business, he'd never had a birth announcement while crafting an obituary!

An obituary is one of those moments when something needs to be announced, timing is important, and there are clear limitations and possibilities that come from the moment. Our joyful news violated expectations for the mortician, who was leading us through the act of crafting one type of announcement, only to hear the opposite.

Ryan was born at 7:30 Monday morning. I went from the hospital in the morning, to the funeral home for the visitation in the afternoon, then back to the hospital to stay overnight. The next morning, I went to the funeral and then back to the hospital later in the afternoon. It was a whipsaw of emotion, and I still remember very little of it besides the strange looks from people at the visitation who hadn't known about the two events happening so close together.

It's amazing how similar condolences and congratulations sound to someone in a daze! People would come up to me and say things like "Well, we can be happy that he's in a better place now," and I'd say "Really? I'm thinking it's a lot colder and noisier than what he's used to." They'd look at me strangely and excuse themselves to go talk with someone who wasn't deranged.

I know that my answers made no sense. They were saying things about death, while I was saying things about life. The things we were saying were appropriate to the occasion; we were just responding to different occasions. Measuring it by Shannon, we would call that a breakdown. But from an oral perspective, we were both saying the right kinds of things for different circumstances.

We can hear this kind of emphasis on the hearer over the speaker in many places in Scripture. The writer of Hebrews discusses the importance of types and foreshadows experienced by Moses in the wilderness, and says this:

> Let us therefore fear, lest, a promise being left us of entering into his rest, any of you should seem to come short of it. For unto us was the gospel preached, as well as unto them: but the word preached did not profit them, not being mixed with faith in them that heard it. (4:1–2)

Notice that the message was the same, but what determined whether the word was powerful was if it was mixed with faith in those who heard it. What was said was far less important than how it was heard. How often do we pray for the speaker, asking for God to anoint and bless what the speaker says? How often do we agonize over how to get our message across, instead of saying, "There are many things I could say to you, but you aren't ready to hear them." That's because the sender/receiver model of communication that underlies our thinking puts the focus on ourselves, and makes what we're saying more important than what we're hearing.

Or consider the passage where Paul describes the whole armor of God. Paul lists the shoes of the preparation of the gospel, the helmet of salvation, the breastplate of righteousness, and the sword of the spirit, and *then* asks his listeners to pray for God to give him something to say that's worth hearing. Instead of starting and stopping with what he should say, Paul makes the utterance an afterthought: pray that the Lord would give me something worth saying and let the Word speak for itself. The message doesn't come from me, it's not novel or new, and the outcome of the word being preached is about transformation, not agreement.

I haven't felt comfortable praying for the minister prior to a sermon in a long time. I can pray that the word they speak will not return void, and will accomplish what it's sent to do. I can pray that the word will be a seed that produces a great tree of faith. I can pray that the word will be the irritant that produces a pearl, and I can pray that the word would divide the thoughts and intents of the hearts of the hearers. I can pray that the word preached would be mixed with faith in the hearer's heart, so that it would benefit the hearer. But I have a hard time praying for the preacher, other than to pray that God would give them utterance that would do what the Lord wants it to do. All of these are about the hearer, not the speaker—what's *heard* instead of what's *said*.

The Shannon model describes a specific kind of messaging, at a certain point in recent history, to people who are users of a specific technology, and who face obstacles that come out of the technology itself. But to generalize this to all people, at all times, in all cultures and historical moments is to retro read. It's to assume that people in the past are just like they are today, only older. To use Shannon's thinking to describe human relationships is to squeeze the life out of them by turning the focus back on the self. Every conversation is an opportunity to attend to the needs of the other person.

When Paul says, "I have determined not to say a word unless it builds up my hearers" (Ephesians 4:29 paraphrase), he's not just speaking idly. It's how he understands the power of his words to serve others. Finally, to use the model to teach how we should improve our relationships and make our friendships and marriage better causes us to look in the wrong place. The emphasis is on whether I'm getting my message across to you and you're agreeing with me, not whether I'm serving you. And at the heart of it, Shannon derived his model while trying to figure out how soldiers could be more efficient at killing people.

There are so many situations where what we say is so much less about being clear, concise, efficient, and accurate, and more about making the right kind of noises to benefit the hearer rather than ourselves.

In short, the modern technological understanding of communication teaches a level of selfishness that permeates the whole relationship. It encourages us to focus on sending messages, to the occlusion of hearing people, and in so doing, it reconstitutes the distance between us and prevents us from the connections we seek. The classical view, which prevailed in the first century, was that communication was the art of discovering what could be the best thing to say in any situation, with the goal of benefiting the hearer.

Modern Views of Relationship Building

The rise of literacy over orality has also changed our definition of relationships and communities, and how we relate to one another. The classical, oral view of language understood the self as embedded in a nexus of relationships that defined the person: I am a son, a father, a husband, a friend, a tradesman in my city, a member of my synagogue, and so forth. If you ask me who I am, I will tell you my nation, my city, my tribe, my family, and my household, like an inverted funnel.

Each of those roles bore responsibilities and expectations, which derive from the community and are clearly conveyed to me throughout my life. I don't choose most of these; they choose me. I follow my father in his profession; I most often live my life in the same town or village in which I was born, and my knowledge and wisdom comes from the elders of my city.

To be completely independent and alone, without a community telling me who I am, isn't something to seek. To be free of the constraints of a community was a frightening prospect. The prodigal son was an example of someone who was completely free from his community's expectations, which was terrifying to the oral thinker. He wasn't free to do what he wanted; he was free from any community who would ground his identity. This terrifying isolation was captured in the statement that no one would give him anything.

To the modern literate thinker, it's the opposite. Descartes's famous statement "I think, therefore I am" is a statement of radical individuality, which asserts that self-awareness and self-definition occur prior to the existence of community. To the oral thinker, "I am because I listen and respond"; to the literate thinker, "I am because I see myself as a separate individual from you, existing prior to human interaction, and transcending your definition of me." In other words, the literate thinker sees the self as existing outside of the community, prior to the community, and after the community. This is in stark contrast to the oral self, which only exists if a community gives it identity. For the literate self to be cut off from their community is almost to be desired—the rite of leaving one's family to become oneself. For the oral thinker, to be cut off from family is to lose identity. Thus, Abraham leaving his family and his household to follow the Lord (Genesis 12) is more than just a covenant leading to the formation of a people; it's a form of self-eradication. He ceases to exist, as far as the community he leaves behind is concerned.

When Abraham leaves his identity to gain a new one, he leaves behind him (in front of him, to be more precise) a hole in the community. For the oral thinker, it was better to be killed in battle than taken as a prisoner, since the dead warrior has an end. We can sing about his bravery in defending the community, his faithfulness to us in giving his own life to protect ours. Even if someone dies, we still sing of him for generations to come. But the warrior who is taken out of his community as a prisoner and sold as a slave has no ending to his story. We can't sing of his ending; we can only end our story with an abrupt loss. Faced with this abrupt loss, the storyteller starts to leave him out of the story, and in time, he simply becomes a footnote.

We can hear this in the story of Enoch as well (Genesis 5). We have no idea what happened to Enoch; we just know that he walked with God, and one day he simply ceased to exist because God took him. We're left to speculate what that means, but there's a sense not only of loss in his ending (he's gone) but of bewilderment (we don't know what happened.) Other than mentioning him in genealogies, we can't say much more about him, so we say very little. Like the warrior who is taken in battle, the abrupt ending leaves us with little to say and no sense of completeness.

We can hear the faint echo of the oral community and self in our parents and grandparents. We've probably all had the experience of mentioning that we saw someone they knew, and then hearing a genealogy lesson:

"I bumped into Julie Smith yesterday, Grandma, and she says hi."

"Who? Oh, yes, isn't her mother Sophie Smith? She was a Pfudzenrueder before she married, and her grandma was a Schlepke. She was a Morton, who married into the Dinglefuss family just about the time that Joey Dinglefuss sold the sick horse to Amos Gunther, which is why the Gunthers never talk with the Smiths at picnics."

Your eyes are rolling, and you have to suppress a yawn. You didn't want a genealogy or a town-gossip lesson; you were just saying that someone remembered her. But what was happening was that Grandma was weaving an identity out of the bits and pieces of other people's stories, in order to arrive at who the person was. You were hearing some very important information on power and influence in the small town too; you just didn't hear it for what it was.

Knapp's Model of Relationship Building

A formal shift in the way theorists defined the community grew out of the redefinition of communication as a technical process. Mark Knapp introduced a model describing how relationships are developed and maintained in 1978. Like the Shannon-Weaver model, this was easily captured in simple visual terms, making it perfect for introductory texts. Like the Shannon model, its terminology and its assumptions permeate our teaching on relationships today. And just like the Shannon model, this one points our attention to some elements of relationships and hides others. Those assumptions need to be questioned and matched against Scripture before we ground our teaching in them. Just like the Shannon model, we may find that we have intuitive understandings that challenge the model.

Mark Knapp described relationships as growing out of the exchange of interpersonal information. Knapp described ten stages of relationships, with five on the side of coming together, and five on the side of coming apart. We've all seen the familiar pyramid showing the names for the levels, and we've all heard about how we move through the stages through the act of self-disclosure. The frequency and the depth of self-disclosure determines the level or name we give to the relationship.[*]

The model looks like this:

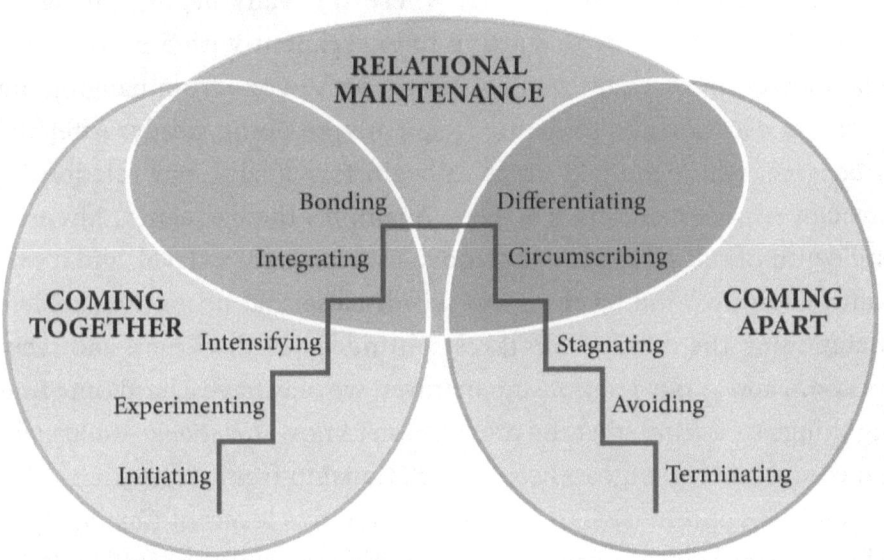

Knapp suggested that we begin with the *Initiating* stage, which is where we know nothing about the other. We disclose something about ourselves that the other person doesn't know—some information that the other person can either accept or reject. It can be an experience, a

---

[*]   Knapp, M. L. (1978). *Social Intercourse: From Greeting to Goodbye.* Allyn and Bacon.

memory, a thought, or an opinion—anything the other person doesn't know about the first person. The other person validates that self-disclosure by sharing something about themselves that the first person doesn't know. A bond begins to form over the reciprocal disclosure of personal information, and life is good.

We may move to the next stage, which is *Experimenting*, by offering some information that's a little more personal and a little more risky. If the disclosure is reciprocated by an equal disclosure, we've moved the relationship to another level. If the information is ignored or not reciprocated, we keep the relationship at the first level. We may never move beyond the first level, or we may stay at the first level for years and then find the opportunity to move it up the pyramid.

The third level is *Integrating*, where we really begin sharing the personal stuff. Now we're starting to experiment with a more formal relationship. In marriage seminar terms, we've gone from hanging out, to dating occasionally, to dating frequently, to going steady. After that is *Bonding*, where we take steps to begin formalizing our relationship through engagement and marriage. Again, it's the frequency, intensity, and depth of self-disclosure that move us from level to level, and it's the continuation of finding things to self-disclose that poses the problem. Maintaining the relationship takes continued self-disclosure and reciprocation, and as our relationship matures, we may have a hard time finding things to disclose that the other doesn't know. *Relational Maintenance* is a continual challenge to keep the relationship from stagnating.

On the opposite side of the pyramid are five levels of *Coming Apart*, where the relationship starts to falter. These five stages are *Differentiating* (we start to see ourselves as separate from the other), *Circumscribing* (we begin to set boundaries around each other's stuff) *Stagnating* (this marriage is going nowhere), *Avoiding* (let's take separate vacations, have separate friends, and live our own lives for a while), and *Terminating* (who gets the kids?).

There are a number of assumptions in this model of relationship building and relational dissolution. First, the model, while useful for describing relationships in general, is often applied to every relationship, as if all relationships are the same. As a result, we use the same model (loosely, of course) to analyze friendships as well as romantic entanglements, workplace conversation as well as life planning, marriages as well as business partnerships. Knapp's model isn't the only theory of relationship development that describes relationships as going through stages, but the language, terminology, and thought behind the model furnishes much of our thinking about relationships in church literature.

While Knapp intended his model to be mostly descriptive, and as a way to analyze and identify the level at which a relationship existed, it's easy to use it prescriptively. It's easy to move from describing how relationships *seem* to develop, to teaching that this is how relationships *should* develop, or that this is what we should do to take a relationship to the next level. We can see how deeply the model has permeated our thinking by the fact that the terms of the model are the way that we describe our relationships in levels.

There are many questions we can ask about the model, and these are really questions about our own relationships. For instance, models of this sort always have a side describing how a relationship forms and grows, and how one stagnates and dies. Knapp finds five stages on each side. But is this a reflection of how things really are in the world, or is this because of the researcher's penchant for symmetry?

A basic rule of math, learned from preschool on, is that if you have five apples on one side of the equal sign, you have to balance it out with five on the other side. And complex models have to be easily visualized when they are reduced to teaching tools. Who would publish an asymmetrical model? Researchers in communication theory use formal methodologies that rely on math for determining validity and, as a result, are more likely to impose symmetry.

The second assumption of the model has to do with the fuel that moves us from one stage to the next, and it's here that we can find ourselves moving away from the first-century thinker. Knapp's model (and other multi-stage models that derive from it) see self-disclosure as the element that moves the model *forward* or *backward*. Relationships that aren't moving in a forward direction have stagnated, and relationships that are falling apart are moving backward. They don't just exist. But relationships have to be moving forward from a beginning point to some goal or ending. They're teleological, not circular.

Self-disclosure is information I share with you that you don't know about me because it's not available to you unless I *choose* to disclose it. I share it as a way of testing the waters, or trying to move the relationship forward. You reciprocate by disclosing something about yourself that I don't know, and that validates my act of risk. All self-disclosure has an element of risk, since it must be validated by a reciprocal act by you.

My risk is that I may disclose something too personal too soon, and you feel that the risk to match it is too great. As long as we remain at a point where we can disclose to each other, we're fine, but if we go beyond, or if continued self-disclosure becomes too risky, the relationship can start to stagnate. I can even make the judgment that the self-disclosure is too much on my side and too little on yours, and I disengage because I'm not getting my needs met. I'm putting more into the relationship than I'm getting out of it, and you're putting in less and getting more.

There have been many refinements to Knapp's model, and other models are covered in early textbooks, but the thinking behind the model stays the same. Interpersonal relationships move through stages of development and are fueled by self-disclosure, sharing information about ourselves that isn't readily available. As long as the information disclosed by one is met with an equal disclosure by the other, the relationship continues to develop. If either stops disclosing because the risk of rejection is greater than the potential reward, the relationship starts to crumble over time.

If this begins to feel like I'm describing a game of poker, it should. There's a big dollop of game theory in models like these, which model human motivation and behavior on the rules of games. Theories like this were developed, in part, as a way of keeping the motive to maximize outcomes and manage risks without having to revert to pure economics. Instead of profit only, which is less clear when applied to complex relationships, game theory eliminates the need to quantify outcomes in purely dollars-and-cents language.

But like a poker game, or any game of cards, there are clear rules to the game. I take my risk based on what I'm holding in my hand, and if what I'm holding doesn't seem like it's enough, then I fold. Sometimes a card player will bluff—that is, pretend that what they hold in their hand is better than it really is. But at some point in the game, we have to lay our cards down and see if we won the hand. This is where our self-image comes in, and where we get moved back to the Johari approach, which looks at our self-concept in light of what others know about us. We make our bets and take our risks based on the judgment of whether our hand is strong enough, and we make that assessment based on who and what we think we are.

If our self-image is distorted, or if we're living in the hidden quadrant, we'll behave in ways that are unhealthy in relation to who we really are. In any event, we are conditioned by models like this to enter every relationship looking for the reason to exit.

Another concept shared by all of these models is the notion of self-disclosure as therapy. Proverbs speaks frequently about holding one's tongue and not telling everything we know. But modern thinking about the self and relationships tells us the opposite: that self-disclosure is the key to relationships, and that *not* disclosing everything about ourselves to others is unhealthy. Self-disclosure and its role in personal and relational health was introduced by Sidney Jourard in 1968.[*]

Based on the work of Carl Rogers, Jourard noticed that his patients were often closed to the world around them, but that they gradually became healthy as they were able to disclose themselves to the therapist. Jourard equated sickness with closedness and health with being open to self-disclosure, a quality which he termed *transparency*. Jourard's explanation inspired much thoughtful work in the area of self-disclosure, all of which developed into a set of assumptions:

1. Disclosure increases with increased relational intimacy.
2. Disclosure increases when rewarded.
3. Disclosure increases with the need to reduce uncertainty in a relationship.
4. Women tend to be higher disclosers than men.
5. Women disclose more with people they like; men disclose more with people they trust.
6. Disclosure is regulated by norms of appropriateness.
7. Attraction is related to positive disclosure but not to negative disclosure.
8. Negative disclosure occurs more frequently in highly intimate settings than in less intimate settings.
9. Satisfaction and disclosure have a curvilinear relationship, so that relational satisfaction is greater at moderate levels of disclosure.[†]

All of these propositions have been studied and tested for decades, with varying degrees of confirmation or refutation, and the outcomes have prompted greater complexity in the range of theories. However, the underlying assumption remains that healthy people disclose information

---

[*] Sidney Jourard, "Disclosing man to himself" (New York: Van Nostrand, 1968.)

[†] Shirley J. Gilbert, "Empirical and Theoretical Extensions of Self-Disclosure," in *Explorations in Interpersonal Communication*, ed. Gerald R. Miller *(Beverly Hills, '976)*

about themselves that others don't know in order to grow and maintain relationships. And the normative nature of theories like Knapp's means that they don't just describe how people develop interpersonal relationships; they are also used to teach us how we *should* act to develop relationships. They are used to tell us what to do if we want our lives and relationships to be better. They have an ideology embedded within them, and it's rare that we are encouraged to question the ideology. That ideology posits that friendships arise out of the reciprocal and commensurate exchange of personal information, based on risk and reward; that healthy people who have friends are healthy *because* they self-disclose; and that unhealthy people don't self-disclose. The notion of transparency further argues that if we don't disclose, we are not telling the truth.

The Impact of Culture on Self-Disclosure

One line of contemporary research looks at the impact of culture on self-disclosure. If we look at the description of self-disclosure in Wikipedia, we find that people in individualist cultures self-disclose as individuals, and that people in collectivist cultures tend to disclose as avatars. This is not surprising, for if we go back to Descartes, we find that defining ourselves as individuals who exist prior to and apart from our community means that we possess information about ourselves that others can't know, and that the only way we can become part of a community is to share that information.

A classical, collectivist, and oral community would see the individual as arising from the roles assigned by the community. You exist as a person because you are already part of a community that knows everything important about you. The need to trade information in order to define who you are, in order to enter into relationships with others, simply doesn't exist.

In a world where your identity is given to you through the community itself, what could I know about myself that you don't already know?

Certainly, details about experiences, wants, and feelings come into play, but they aren't the currency through which we define ourselves. It's only through literacy that the modern self comes into being, because the possibility exists that I can show you one person while I construct another self in writing.

In a highly connected, online world, we don't exist unless we are posting intimate details about our lives in order to define ourselves to ourselves and to others. We aren't considered healthy if we aren't posting, or if we say we are fine when we are not. We aren't healthy unless we're sending messages to followers with little thought of sharing meaning. We have gone from "I am because my community gives me identity," to "I have identity and existence because I think," to "I exist because I'm sending messages."

Our connected culture has moved from having identity to speaking at all times in order to *find* our identity. In some sad ways, we now speak not to share, but to shout into an echo chamber so we can even exist. We've gone from "I am, therefore I think" to "I think, therefore I am" to "I share memes, therefore I am." In short, modern communication is the act of sending messages about myself to confirm my own thinking, and health comes out of disclosing everything about me.

If this description seems extreme, consider the lyrics to two recently popular songs by well-known Christian artists. In one listeners hear that telling someone you are fine in response to a casual greeting is lying, not admitting secrets and wounds is deception, and that the only way to fix being out of control is being honest.

These lyrics echo many of the tenets of a modern therapeutic view of language. First, the self is behind closed doors, alone and inside. We "reach out" to someone because we're inside something. Second, telling someone that everything is fine, even when it's not, is lying. The truth is seldom told, but when it is told, it fixes things. In fact, the only way to repair the brokenness is to disclose what you don't want others to know about yourself.

This is a cry to heal yourself at the same time that you find your true self, and it invokes the notion of *authenticity* as revealing an inner self full of warts and rough edges. These lyrics echo the modern notion that relationships depend on self-disclosure, that there's both great risk and potential reward to be gained by being honest and telling everything, and that withholding authenticity is deception. Even a casual response (fine) to the casual question "How are you doing?" is inauthentic and a lie in this framework. In fact, this song tells us that we are seldom honest, making honesty the exception rather than the rule.

In another song, which was nominated for a Grammy in 2014, we can hear again the assumptions of talk as therapy. The key to relationships between each other, and between ourselves and God, is found in honesty and self-disclosure. Being open and sharing everything bad about ourselves is being honest, while not sharing everything is being dishonest. Lack of self-disclosure builds walls between ourselves trapped "in here" in darkness while leaving you alone "out there." Self-disclosure, despite its risks, is worth it, because it sets us free, it brings us God's love, it changes our lives, and it invites and even triggers the mercy of God. Thus, self-disclosure is more than a tool to build relationships; it brings mercy, healing, and belonging. In short, unless I tell you everything about myself, I'm lying to you, and I'm not the person I was created to be.[*]

But experience tells us that this view of relationships doesn't make sense and can't be sustained. We all intuitively know that sharing intimate details of our lives with strangers can be selfish and inappropriate. Even those

---

[*]   In an earlier draft, I'd included the lyrics to both songs, but I've chosen to omit them because the barriers to quoting were insurmountable. The visual marks that represent the sounds of the thoughts sung by the first person to sing them are owned by multiple companies and individuals, and to show you those squiggles without paying the companies violates copyright. The very act of making squiggles of any kind on my computer screen is potentially violating laws if someone else made the same squiggles in the same order and then claimed ownership rights. Like Paul, who didn't know sin until the law came, every act of writing creates possible violations of copyright. Perhaps that's why we write in sentences!

who make their living posing on social media express outrage if their personal space is violated. We've all experienced the person who turns every conversation, no matter how casual, into an outpouring of their problems. There are limits to what we feel comfortable hearing about others, and we consider those who know how much to share, at what moments and in what settings, to have gained some maturity and perspective. And how does this view of healthy relationships carry out James's admonition "Everyone should be quick to hear, and slow to speak?" (James 1:19)

What I find most interesting about the whole notion of equating self-disclosure with honesty, and withholding information with dishonesty, is that it echoes the story of the temptation in the Garden of Eden.

> Now the serpent was more subtle than any beast of the field which the LORD God had made. And he said unto the woman, Yea, hath God said, Ye shall not eat of every tree of the garden? And the woman said unto the serpent, We may eat of the fruit of the trees of the garden: But of the fruit of the tree which *is* in the midst of the garden, God hath said, Ye shall not eat of it, neither shall ye touch it, lest ye die. And the serpent said unto the woman, Ye shall not surely die: For God doth know that in the day ye eat thereof, then your eyes shall be opened, and ye shall be as gods, knowing good and evil. (Genesis 3:1–5)

Listen to the tempter's appeal: "There's something that God's not telling you, something He's holding back. Because He hasn't told you everything, He's lying to you. You won't die; in fact, knowing this will change your life by making you more like Him. You'll know the difference between good and evil." Isn't it interesting that the first temptation in the garden contained the same appeal as every multi-level marketing scheme, every confidence scheme, every insider trading scheme, and every article about using authenticity as a tool to sell more widgets?

Just yesterday, I came across two articles that exemplify the extent to which our culture has embraced the notion that our self is inside of us, that communication consists of sending the right messages to others outside of us and sending the right kind of self-disclosing messages. But these articles go to an uncomfortable extreme: they assert that our businesses will not be successful if we aren't self-disclosing authentically. In so many words, they assert that unless we disclose completely and authentically, our customers will think we're lying and not buy our services.

The writers can't really tell us what authenticity is, or how our audiences can discern authenticity outside of the gift of discernment, but in their view, authentic self-disclosure is the key to success in every business relationship. They also echo the belief that the true self lies inside of us and can only be seen by our being open and honest with each other. Thus, we "speak out," we "lash out," and we "reach out," all metaphors of interiority of the self, and all echoing the notion that to speak is to "connect." Or, as I hear constantly on Christian radio and in sermons, echoing the need to "plug in." Modern headlines don't tell me what the subject of a story may have said. They "reveal the real reason that..." or they "finally reveal..." as if these things were hidden until the reporter ferreted them out. Every utterance is "revealed" and every true reason is discerned ("the real reason that such and such happened") by the writer.

The same thinking permeates the materials we use in our courses on relationships, in our popular songs, in our worship services, and in our prayer lives. We believe that we (our selves) exist prior to and separate from our community, and that the function of communication is to bridge the gap by sending the right kind of messages to others and to God. Unless we trade personal information for others' personal information, and do so authentically, we remain alone and unwell. In modern terms, we're all broken, which has replaced the notion of missing the mark. The Lord came, we tell each other, not to rescue us from the death that results from sin, but to heal our broken hearts.

And that is the essence of modern friendship today. We teach that a friend is someone with whom we've traded personal information at a breadth and depth that is both risky and authentic. We don't really know and can't really describe what authentic is, but we're sure we can detect what it isn't. Like sincerity, energy, or charisma, authenticity is an undefinable quality that makes or breaks the relationship. Authentic self-disclosure (if we take the lyrics at face value) heals our brokenness, releases mercy, sets us free, and is what we are destined to be.

Oral Culture's View on Friendship

But does this describe how oral cultures think about the self, language, and relationship? Would oral cultures believe that the self is always trapped inside of the body, existing separate from and apart from the community? And that having endless phone conversations where we send messages to others is how we discover who we are, join communities, and even heal ourselves? That the function of communication always comes back to me in the singular? My meaning? My message? My "speaking out?" My self-discovery? My healing? My gain in trading secrets? Or would they be more comfortable seeing relationships growing out of the concern for the community before the self, where using words to defuse the other's pain or to celebrate the other person's good fortune would be the right thing to do? Where saying the right kinds of things, appropriate to the situation and the moment, is more important than sending a message about the speaker? Where we can rejoice with those who rejoice and mourn with those who mourn because the community is more important than my own needs?

Classical writers (and there are many) explored friendship, but not as much as they focused on the mechanisms whereby friendships were built. They chose to explore why friendships were made, and the different types that could be entered into. Aristotle, for instance, described friendships in one of three categories: friendships of utility, friendships of pleasure, and friendships of virtue.

The first, utility, came about because working together to accomplish something was necessary. We could become friends with someone over tasks and purposes, because we were mutually useful to each other. The second was enjoyed solely because of the pleasure to be found in having a friend. The third, virtue, was because close association with someone who was regarded as virtuous brought about virtue in the other. We become friends because we are mutually beneficial to each other.[*]

In the first century BCE, Cicero described the mutual benefit to be found in friendships. His book was presented as a transcript of a conversation about friendship, not an internal analysis of the concept. His speakers discussed the mutual benefits to be found in each type of friendship, the need for friendships, the obligations of friendships, and the ultimate end of friendships, which was the pursuit of virtue. Classical thinkers questioned whether men could be friends with women; if men could be friends with equals, superiors, or inferiors; and if friendship truly existed if financial gain was an outcome of the relationship. They questioned if someone could be a friend because the relationship was compelled by authority. But overall, the emphasis remained on the mutual nature of the association, and the benefits to be found by both.

An asymmetrical friendship, where one derived something while the other didn't, wasn't considered a true friendship. And the friendship was not a vehicle of self-discovery or self-validation, but it was about mutual benefit in pursuit of virtue. Friendship wasn't about one person getting something from another by exchanging; it was about the one person benefiting the other. True friendship is rare, to be valued, and to be sought after and cultivated as a necessary part of the whole person in their journey through life.

---

[*]   *Ethics*, 8:3–4

The book of Proverbs stands in this tradition, and while the Old Testament treatment of friendship is always demonstrated through story rather than analyzed in writing, it has much to add to our understanding of the classical world. Saul Olyan suggests that the story of Ruth and Naomi demonstrates all of the characteristics of classical friendship, which is a very important contribution from Hebrew thought.[*] Other sources and traditions from antiquity ignore women's friendships altogether.

To summarize, modern friendship is based on the number of connections we have—the number of followers and people we influence. These are people who are mostly unknown to us, but we base our status in the world on their opinion as expressed on our Twitter or Instagram pages. In modern friendship, distance is baked in, leaving is baked in, and opinion rules the day. Online friendships raise the risk of rejection to a certainty. Finally, we regard friendships as if they are machines that can break, needing to be fixed or patched. They're tenuous at best, transitory in nature, and fraught with danger. Like all modern relationships, friendship is unstable, and in constant danger of unraveling if it's not fed a constant diet of self-disclosure.

---

[*] Saul M. Olyan, *Friendship in the Hebrew Bible. (New Haven: Yale University Press,* 2017), 85.

The Tension Between Two Worlds:
Communication and Leadership

Ephesians 4:29 says, "Let no unwholesome word proceed from your mouth, but only such as word as is good for edification, according to the need of the moment, so that it will give grace to those who hear."

1. Is the ultimate goal to get a message across without distortion, or is it to build up the hearer?

2. Where is the focus; on the speaker, or on the hearer? On what is said, or what is heard?

3. Is the message a response to the moment (exigence) or is it a great idea from the speaker's mind?

4. Is the determinant of wholesome vs. unwholesome whether the speaker is understood, or whether the hearer is edified?

5. If we begin with a focus on the hearer, respond only to the need in an appropriate timeframe and using the possible resources of the moment, and measure its utility by whether it accomplishes the goal of the meeting the hearer's need, does it matter what we say? Or is it more important that we say the right *kind* of things in the right timing with the right intent?

For consideration: This suggests that unwholesome words aren't necessarily profanity, but that unwholesome words can be any words that don't build up the hearer. NO attention is given to the speaker or their message outside of their ability to discern the need and the moment. In other words, all speaking is rooted in community needs and community judgment.

6. How would this change your understanding of sermon prep?

7.   Would it change how you pray about your sermons?

8.   Would it change how you pray publicly for speakers and teachers?

The Tension Between Two Worlds: Self and Community

In I Corinthians 12, Paul uses the metaphor of a body to describe the church. We are made to be part of one body by Christ; we are born into that body, none of us have a separate existence, and our function in the body is our identity.

1. How does the community existing before the self, and the self arising from its function in the community, differ from the self existing before and separate from the community?

2. How do you reconcile the tension between the modern self (I exist because I tweet) to the ancient self (I only exist because I'm part of a community)?

3. If Paul is speaking to a collective rather than to a group of isolated but overlapping selves, would it change how we hear his comments about destiny, purpose, and calling?

4. The modern world has embraced the idea of narrative, but only in the singular. How would you teach about our identity coming from OUR story rather than a bunch of individual stories that overlap?

5. How would teaching about identity coming *from* the community change how we teach and lead our faith communities?

6. Are there any Scriptures that you struggle to explain that sound different when heard through a collective ear? How would you teach those ideas differently in the echo of orality?

6

The Audacity of Friendship

In the last chapter, we discussed modern Western views on the self, and the nature and role of communication in relationship building. The modern Western view of the self is pre-existing the community and apart from the community, while the role of communication is to shape the thoughts and actions of others to comport with and validate the individual's intent. We saw that modern relationships are built on the exchange of personal information, in an escalating risk game that carries its own rules and triggers for how the relationship can come apart. Finally, we saw how language itself is viewed as representational—that is, a continual reference to something else rather than a force in itself.

Shannon's model is about information transfer in a mechanistic environment. It's not about human relationships, but about power: the means to make you think like me. And Knapp's model is about how we exchange guarded messages to create relationships that have the same intrinsic value, whether a formal business relationship or a romantic one. Add in the notion that equates self-disclosure with honesty, which brings freedom and health, while not trading personal information is dishonest and sick, and we put tremendous pressure on all of our relationships. But is this the way that people in Jesus' day would have heard the invitation to friendship?

When Jesus called His disciples "friends," was He inviting them into the modern set of assumptions that describe our twenty-first century relationships with ourselves and others? And when we invite others to have a relationship with Him, is this the kind of relationship we should be seeking? What would Jesus's listeners have heard when He made the invitation?

A few years ago, David Konstan wrote a fascinating book called *Friendship in the Classical World.* In it, he traced the complex meanings of friendship in the Hellenistic period and beyond through the first three centuries. Konstan shows that, far from it being the exchange of inter-personal information with the goal of self-validation and self-healing, friendship had very specific meanings that had to do with promises and obligations to others.

While the texts of the period were written, they were not done so from the same literate mindset we talked about earlier. Rather, they are texts written to capture the result of oral disputation and discussion. They are transcripts of dictation, captured between a speaker and a hearer, describing dialogues with other philosophers. They show all of the elements and sensitivities of oral thinkers. Like the epistles, they were spoken to a scribe, who wrote what was said in order to make it spoken to others who received it. And as we saw with Augustine, the ability to read silently was taken as a mark of genius more than three hundred years after Paul dictated his letters.

To call someone a friend in Jesus' day was to make a pledge of obligation for mutual benefit. It was, in part, to pledge access to your resources for the other's benefit. And while the details of those pledges are the subject of robust debate among ancient thinkers, there were common elements that all incorporated into their descriptions.

To call someone a friend was, first, to *declare* that something existed, not just to put a label on a relationship that already existed. It was to act verbally by declaring it to be so, not to acknowledge what already was. To call someone a friend was a *presentational* utterance, not a *representational* utterance. Just as we declare a couple to be married, or we declare a student to be graduated, a presentational utterance changes reality by bringing into existence what didn't exist before. We declare a thing to be so, and it is.

Three Promises or Pledges

To declare a friendship was to make three promises or pledges:
1. I take pleasure in your company.
2. What's mine is yours.
3. I'm dedicated to helping you work toward the good, the cultivation of virtue.

These three, taken together, create a bond far stronger than just a community that gives me an identity and locates me in the world. A declaration of friendship places everything I have at your disposal. On the flip side, the declaration "I am not your friend" cuts off the other person from access to help or assistance.

The first declaration, "I find pleasure in your company," seems to be the easiest of the three for us modern Westerners to grasp. "I simply enjoy being with you. Not because I can get something, and not because I can give you something. At this point, I simply enjoy being around you. I'm not using you to validate myself or to heal myself, but to simply relax and enjoy being with you. Like Mary, I'm content to simply sit with you, not making the relationship work for something, but simply to be."

The second is a little tougher to grasp. I'm putting everything I have at your disposal. No need to ask, no need to beg; just take it if you need it. I once had a friend challenge me when I asked if I could borrow a tool to use on a home improvement project. When I asked, he said, "No. You know better than to *ask* me. You just *tell* me you're going to stop by and pick it up for a while." I was shocked for a moment, until I realized that he was saying friends don't need to ask as if they're apologizing. There's no need to ask, because permission has already been given. They only need to say that they're exercising the permission. I may still ask, but it's really just a courtesy in case you had plans for what I need.

This second element, "What's mine is yours," is what modern thinkers gravitate toward when asked to describe a childhood friendship. We don't describe friendships as exchanges of information, but as sharing everything we have and having the confidence that the other person will share everything as well. Instead of self-disclosure as a means of healing ourselves, we see sharing of secrets as a privilege. But something tragic happens as we grow older and are taught the modern view of relationships: we leave them behind.

Sometimes this just happens because interests diverge as we discover our educational or career paths, and sometimes this is because we simply move away. But it's interesting to note that the fading of childhood friendships begins at just about the same time that we begin to learn about the finer points of communication and relationships in our English classes. Some even argue that we are *taught* to leave childhood friendships, and even forced to leave them, in favor of shallow relationships built on mechanistic information-exchange models.

The third declaration, "I'm dedicated to helping you work toward the good, the cultivation of virtue," is the hardest for us postmodern literate thinkers to grasp. We're heavily influenced by dualism—the belief that something is either this or that, but not both at the same time. For us, things are either good or bad, light or dark, positive or negative, body or spirit. We place heavier emphasis on what our senses can discern, and then categorize them as either this or that. Sometimes, the extremes we take can seem absurd.

For instance, is the earth young or old? We can spend careers and lifetimes arguing for one over the other, thinking that if our view doesn't prevail, everything falls. We don't notice that none of the New

Testament writers bothered to ask or answer the same question. They may have used Creation in a general sense as proving the existence of God, or the story of the Fall in the garden as a demonstration of human nature, but they never bothered to ask if it was literally true. Of course, this is in part because *literally* and *figuratively* didn't carry the same weight as they do today. To be "literally true" depends on whether the written account has been independently tested and proven by other written sources.

For modern thinkers, *good* or *bad* are categories of judgment. Thinkers of Jesus' day instead spoke of *the good*, not just *good*. *The good* was similar to what we'd call practical wisdom: the ability to know the midpoint between too much and too little in any given situation. Another way this gets translated is *moderation*. Like all of the virtues, this was not a characteristic that one *possessed*, but was demonstrated in the way one *acted*. In fact, the person couldn't possess characteristics at all until the individual was invented centuries later.

Think of it this way: until we can separate you from your words through writing, and examine if your words are consistent with your character, we can't see inside of you to see what you really are. We can only see the way you act and judge if it's consistent with what our community would expect under the given circumstances. We can't say you *are* brave, but we can say that you acted *bravely*. We can't say that you are loyal, but we can say that you *acted* loyally according to what our peers would expect in a situation like this. We can't say that you *are* generous, but we can say that you *acted* generously. We can't judge that you are *kind*, but we can say that you *acted* kindly according to our laws and expectations.

For example, look at how David is described in 1 Samuel 18:12–16:

> And Saul was afraid of David, because the LORD was with
> him, and was departed from Saul. Therefore Saul re-
> moved him from him, and made him his captain over a

thousand: and he went out and came in before the people. And David behaved himself wisely in all his ways: and the LORD was with him. Wherefore when Saul saw that he behaved himself very wisely, he was afraid of him. But all Israel and Judah loved David, because he went out and came in before them.

Later translations, which don't retain the oral nature of the KJV, give us this: "In everything he did he had great success, because the LORD was with him. When Saul saw how successful he was, he was afraid of him" (vv. 14–15 NIV).

Notice two things: "he acted wisely" is now "success," which shifts our attention from actions that we could see and evaluate within the expectations of a community, to characteristics and outcomes that David *possesses*. Success has become an *internal* part of his character rather than a pattern of behavior that we judge. The comparison is not his behavior against the backdrop of a community, but the comparison of his outcomes against other people's outcomes.

Knowing David has shifted from our assigning a positive judgment of his actions to our assessing his internal character. There's also the tantalizing repetition of the way he "came in and went out" before the people. Again, this is an evaluation we make of David's actions against the backdrop of our expectations. The modern translation simply tells us that "he led the troops in their campaigns." The modern translation tells us the simple fact that he led the troops, while "coming in and going out" may have a different resonance altogether. In a future book, we'll explore the significance of the phrase and its repetition in this and other places in Scripture. The modern eye might be missing what the ancient ear was hearing!

In part, this is because until the invention of the independent self, there wasn't really a sense that there could be a difference between your words and actions and your identity. Think of it this way. Words are transient. They disappear as soon as we speak them, unless we have some means of recording them, either aurally or through a kind of short-hand marks that make a record of what was said. Either way of making a record changes what was said from an event in time to an object that can be handled, stored, and referred back to at some future point in time. Until I can turn your words into an object that can be studied, I can't compare your words to your actions beyond recent memory, and I can't compare your words today to your words yesterday. I can't study your words for evidence of character, and thus, I can't speak of your character as separate from you. Your words are actions, not clues to the "real" you who is hidden inside of you.

I can look at whether your words and other sorts of actions are within what the community expects of its members in this type of situation. I can act and speak in such a way as to invite your judgment of my character. As a result, ancient oral thinkers focused on developing virtues, which consisted of identifying the middle ground between too much and too little of a response within the laws and customs of a community. For instance, one of the virtues was generosity, or the willingness to share what one had with those who had need.

Rather than saying that a person *was* generous, we'd say that a person *acted* generously because their response to a need was to give what was neither too much nor too little according to the laws and customs of the community. One could give too little, or one could give too much, and both could be seen by the harm that would be caused—either to the person in need or to the family of the giver who gave too much. The midpoint between too much and too little was termed *the good*, and that was the point of practical wisdom that was cultivated and studied.

For the Greeks, the goal of cultivating the virtues was *phronesis*, and the person who exhibited *the good* in all things was called *phronimos*, the practical wise person who understood what was appropriate in all circumstances and situations. This type of wisdom is different from *sophia*, which tended more toward knowledge and understanding attained by learning from others who were wiser. To be judged as phronimos was a lifelong quest, and the highest goal of a Greek education. To be sure, the Greek philosophers weren't the only ones to have a concept like this, and they weren't the only ones to capture their thinking about virtue in writing. But their dialogues constituted the bulk of what a young Roman citizen like Paul would have studied, and that shaped the thoughts of those to whom Paul preached the gospel.

Paul contrasts the wisdom of men with the wisdom of God, but he seldom uses the term *phronimos*, and then in a derisive way. For instance, in 1 Corinthians 4:10, he says "We are fools for Christ, but you are so wise in Christ! We are weak, but you are strong! You are honored, we are dishonored!" (NIV). An oral thinker would have heard the mocking statement "you think we apostles are stupid, while you Corinthians are the epitome of Greek erudition and sophistication. You are so wise."

Jesus, on the other hand, uses the term in a complimentary way—to describe the wise virgins (Matthew 5), the wise steward (Matthew 24), and the wise servant (Matthew 24). It's the term He uses when He tells His followers to be wise as serpents and harmless as doves (Matthew 10:16). In Jesus' use, this is wisdom that is seen in action, where the standards for judgment are taken from the circumstances. In the epistles, Paul admonishes his followers to let their moderation be known in all things. John tells us that the mark of the believer is love, while Paul tells us that it's our moderation (practical wisdom grounded in community expectations) that testifies to the Greeks.

Some scholars see a reference to the difference between orality and literacy in Paul's discussion of the superiority of God's wisdom and the linking of God's wisdom to proclamation. One of the ongoing disputes among Hellenistic thinkers was whether writing an idea on paper reduced its claim to truth. One could question a person making a statement, but a text couldn't be questioned. One could question the writer as to intent and meaning, but again, this wasn't in the text. It was only commentary on the statement.

Once written down, it became an object all its own, and no one could speak for its meaning and intent. In a courtroom, a statement could be witnessed, but again, a statement couldn't be questioned. In short, once written down, an idea became only a record or facsimile of a statement of truth, not the truth itself. Thus, truth claims contained in writing were men's wisdom, while truth claims in the oral, that could be questioned and disputed, had the potential to rise above men's wisdom.

It's fascinating to note that Paul's letters were dictated to university towns in Roman cities, and that he began those letters by raising the issue of the nature of truth and wisdom in those letters. In the dispute, Paul sided with truth and power of the gospel residing in the oral over the written. In opposing God's wisdom to man's wisdom, Paul isn't comparing written statement to written, with some written statements containing God's truth and others containing men's truth. He's comparing written statements (men's wisdom) to oral statements (proclaiming in the oral). In short, prophets speak, while philosophers are slowly coming to rely on the written over the oral. Some modern historians even see the dispute between Paul and John to be this very issue, with Paul choosing the oral, while John's Gospel takes written form, with many of the early characteristics of written narrative form.

The third element of friendship was thus a commitment to the other to do whatever was necessary to help your friend work out "the good." To call someone a friend was to make a declaration to that person, and anyone else within hearing, that "First, I take pleasure in being with you. I just enjoy hanging out, not to get something, but because you're enjoyable to be around. Second, what's mine is yours. If you need it, and I have it, take it, without question or excuse. Third, I'm committing everything I am and have to helping you work out balance, moderation, and practical wisdom in every part of your life. That promise extends to you and to your children as well." It is why Proverbs tells us to go to our father's friend in times of trouble instead of our brother. There's a commitment to help that transcends the life of the original promise and even goes beyond the bond of family. Given the frequent animosity that we see between the firstborn and the second born in Scripture, that shouldn't be surprising.

But notice something very important here: this type of relationship focuses on what I can do and be for you, not what you offer to me. It isn't built on an exchange of personal information that ultimately serves my interest. This friendship is based on a commitment that focuses on you first. Unlike modern friendship, it really isn't about me at all, other than the reciprocal commitment that you make back to me. This kind of commitment can happen only between equals, not between unequals.

It's important to note that this sense of *friend* is what the Greeks used to describe treaties and agreements between sovereign nations. It's a relationship of mutual support and interest, which places both under very deep commitments of aid and help. In Deuteronomy 23:6, Moses tells the Israelites, "Do not seed a treaty of friendship with them as long as you live" (NIV), because of the obligations of material and military aid it would create. (Wait…did Moses just refer to a treaty as something organic, which grows from planting, instead of a written document?)

Oral cultures used another term for this kind of relationship: *face-to-face*. One could stand face-to-face only in this kind of bond with an equal sovereign. It was a special kind of standing, reserved for just a few in life because of the depth of the commitment. Exodus 33:11 tells us, "The LORD would speak to Moses face to face, as one would speak to a friend" (NIV), telling us a great deal about the depth of their relationship. The fact that only a few people would be named friends in Scripture also suggests that Jesus' hearers would recognize how unique the invitation was to enter into friendship with the Almighty.

Psalm 55:12–14 expresses the depth of sorrow that comes when a friend betrays a friend. This psalm is often regarded as a prophetic description of Judas betraying Jesus.

> For it was not an enemy that reproached me; then I could have borne it: neither was it he that hated me that did magnify himself against me; then I would have hid myself from him: But it was thou, a man mine equal, my guide, and mine acquaintance. We took sweet counsel together, and walked unto the house of God in company.

Modern translations (e.g., the ESV) say, "But it is you, a man my equal, my companion, my familiar friend."

Face-to-face can even describe an enemy for whom one has great respect, a notion that was captured and expressed by Rudyard Kipling in "The Ballad of East and West":

> Oh, East is East, and West is West, and never the twain shall meet,

> Till Earth and Sky stand presently at God's great Judgment Seat; But there is neither East nor West, Border, nor Breed, nor Birth, When two strong men stand face to face, though they come from the ends of the earth!*

The poem, published in 1889, tells the story of a confrontation between a British soldier and an indigenous leader in Pakistan, who start out as mortal enemies but end up becoming blood brothers through a lengthy chase and confrontation. The mutual respect that they have for each other transcends their enmity, and they eventually swear an oath of friendship at the cost of life itself. As such, it captures some of the differences between a literate culture and an oral culture when one invades the other.

---

* Rudyard Kipling's Verse (Definitive Edition). (Garden City, NY: Doubleday) 233-236

These three commitments, or declarations, constitute a mature friendship in the oral culture of the hearers of the gospel: "I take pleasure in your company. What's mine is yours, and I'm committed to helping you work out balance, moderation, and practical wisdom in all areas of your life." Not, "I'll be your friend if you accept and respect the bits of information I disclose to you, and you'll reciprocate by sending back similar information about yourself, until the risk of rejection overcomes the desire for connection." And it's the first that Jesus offers us, not the second. The second comes out of defining the human in terms of a technology, and then teaching ourselves that the technology is what we should emulate.

Friendship with Jesus

Imagine that Jesus was offering us a modern notion of friendship when He called us friends. What can we possibly tell Him about our-selves that He doesn't already know? If He knows everything about us, having formed us, having redeemed us, and then having ordered our steps by guiding us through the events that shape our character, what can we tell Him that He doesn't know far better than us? And if the cur-rent model of friendship is to be pursued, is there a point already built into the relationship from the beginning where it's acceptable for Him to leave it?

"I will never leave you nor forsake you" and "I am with you always" doesn't sound like "I'm not getting enough out of this exchange to keep it at its current level. My needs aren't being met. So I'm going to find someone who accepts me for who I tell them I am." Just as the phrase "He's never failed me *yet*" includes the possibility that He might fail me this time or in the future, the modern notion of friendship always holds the threat of terminating.

What might this invitation have sounded like to an oral thinker in Jesus' day? "Are you saying that you take pleasure in my company? That you simply enjoy being with me? The Master and Maker of the universe enjoys hanging out with His creation? That just as you sought out Adam to walk with your voice in the cool of the garden, you seek out my presence to enjoy? What a stunning thought, Lord, that *you* would want to hang out with *me!*"

I've been taught all of my life that it's the other way around. I have to seek His presence, and He's very temperamental and flighty. My years of listening to adults drop into their prayer voices, as if God is four years old and hard of hearing ("O Lord, we do humbly...and hesitantly...seek your face...and thank you for this thy....great bounty...") underscores the importance of my trying my best to impress Him. But the incarnation teaches me the lengths to which *He* will go to clear the way for me to know Him. And we know that we didn't choose Him; He chose us.

The second element, "what's mine is yours," is much easier for us to grasp, but not in the fullness of an oral world. We know that everything we need has been provided, and that He's promised to meet our every need. But we still teach ourselves that His provision is based on our efforts to please Him. We don't feel that if we need it and He has it, it's there for our use without even having to ask.

I'll go out on another limb here and suggest that we spend more time and effort within Christian circles arguing about how we're supposed to regard material blessing than most other topics. We range from the belief that God wants us to be successful and blessed to the opposite view that God wants us poor and humble so we can identify with the poorest in our world. But somewhere in the middle, we all believe that He has provided all that we need to live the lives He's called us to live. No matter how much we might try to explain away hardship or blessing, we still believe that God is good and generous.

How about the third element of the promise of friendship: the pledge of helping the other grow in practical wisdom and understanding? Is He offering to commit all that He has to helping me come to maturity and wholeness in Him? That I might come to the fullness of the measure of a man or woman? Obviously, yes, His actions toward us from Creation on show that His desire for us is to grow up in Him. Our songs proclaim that He's good.

There are two elements of this classical understanding of friendship that are hard to grasp from the perspective of modern thinking. The first is that He'd take pleasure in my company. The second is that by declaring a friendship, He's inviting me to make the same commitments to Him as a sovereign equal: to stand face-to-face with Him for all the world to see. It's easy for us to proclaim that we take pleasure in His company, and it's not so hard for us to say that what's mine is His. It's harder to grasp how I could commit my best to helping Him work out balance, moderation, and practical wisdom in His life. But recall the times that He asked His disciples to do as He was doing, to preach the gospel and feed His sheep, to teach and minister to His followers wherever they may be. Our commitment to help Him work out phronesis is in His Body, among His followers.

Classical vs. Modern Friendship

The biggest difference between this classical understanding of friendship and our modern understanding is the focus. Modern friendship is all about me: what I get out of the relationship, how I benefit or lose, and how the friendship affects me. Everything is about "empowerment," which is indicative of feeling powerless. Classical friendship, on the other hand, is about *you*. I take pleasure in your company; what I have is there for *your* use, and I stand ready help to *you* grow and mature. Nothing is about me except what I offer to you.

And therein lies the biggest source of satisfaction: joy comes in giving, not getting. Because my threshold changes from day to day, what satisfies me today won't be enough tomorrow, and eventually you won't be able to fill it for me. That's one big reason that modern friendships are so empty; they're all about me, if I've learned to understand them through the exchange model.

The story of the prodigal son grows in breadth as we hear something echoed in the father's treatment of both the elder and the younger son. The father takes pleasure in both sons, in spite of the radical difference in their actions. That doesn't change when the son comes home in disgrace. The father runs to him when he sees him. Clearly, the younger son has come to believe that the father really means that what he has is there for the son's use.

The father demonstrates this when he gives the second son his inheritance at the son's request. When the elder son objects to the father's welcome of the younger son home, the father tells him, "You are always with me, and everything I have is yours." There are many lessons to be taken from the story, but one unique element that only an oral culture would hear is that the father was really exemplifying the offer of friendship by the way he treated the sons—the younger by his act of giving him what he asked for, and the elder by pointing out that he can only see himself as a slave (not even a servant) in spite of what he could have had.

The younger son is keenly aware of the distinctions in their relationships when he realizes that even a servant is better off than a poor beggar. In his remorse, he intends to ask his father's forgiveness and to be treated as a servant, but the father stands with him face-to-face for all to see and again puts what he has at the son's disposal. That he takes pleasure in the son's return is obvious by his celebration.

What is most striking about this hearing is that the younger son is finally able to enter into the friendship that's been offered by the father to both sons, while the elder isn't. The younger son has been restored by the father's forgiveness, while the elder son can only see himself as a slave working for land and cattle upon which he has no claim and that he doesn't own. And while the younger son has wasted his portion of the father's estate, he has truly grown into accepting the relationship that the father seeks, making all he's spent worth it.

I daresay that the father wasn't surprised by the son's use of the money, and that he cared less for the money than for the younger son's growth and maturity. In that sense, giving the younger son what he asked for while knowing that the son would probably waste it may have been helping him work out wisdom. Much like we might hand our teenagers the keys to our car, knowing there might be a scratch or two, and knowing it might end up somewhere in a snow bank some dark winter night, but knowing that it's part of the process of maturing, this father was able to see beyond the risk of material loss to what was best for the son.

This father carried through on the commitment to give all that he had to help his son grow in practical wisdom. That the younger son got there first is the surprising part of the story, and the part of the parable that means the most to me. It's not the one who exhibits dutiful behavior and hard work while seething about the injustice of their treatment; it's the one who can take the risk, confident that the father means what he says, and knowing underneath it all that he can be forgiven his failures, who is pleasing to God. It's the audacity of the younger son that irritates the older brother—the audacity of believing that he can enter into friendship with his father instead of remaining only an obedient son.

Jesus asked His disciples about the audacity that friendship entails in Luke 11:5–10:

> Which of you shall have a friend, and shall go unto him at midnight, and say unto him, Friend, lend me three loaves; For a friend of mine in his journey is come to me, and I have nothing to set before him? And he from within shall answer and say, Trouble me not: the door is now shut, and my children are with me in bed; I cannot rise and give thee. I say unto you, Though he will not rise and give him, because he is his friend, yet because of his importunity he will rise and give him as many as he needeth.

> And I say unto you, Ask, and it shall be given you; seek, and ye shall find; knock, and it shall be opened unto you. For every one that asketh receiveth; and he that seeketh findeth; and to him that knocketh it shall be opened.

This is more than just a parable; it's the disciples being challenged by a direct question. It's not Jesus saying, "Once upon a time…"; it's Him asking, "What would you do if…" using the disciples' own friendships as a way of challenging their beliefs about the Father's faithfulness.

If we see Jesus' question through the eyes of literacy, we come away believing that the point of the question is persistence in the face of someone who has what I need but doesn't want to get his butt out of bed to give it to me. The point of persistence is to keep asking after I've been given poor excuses for not acting (the door is shut; my kids are in bed). So if I need something, I can go to God, who doesn't really want to help me out, and if I keep bugging Him about it, He'll finally stop giving me poor excuses and give me what I demand.

Since this doesn't preach very well, we invented context so that God doesn't come out of this discussion looking bad. We say that He's testing us to see if we really want it, or He's teaching us persistence, or that the person was concerned about thieves and didn't want to open the door. Even if this is culturally true, it still reinforces the lesson that God's provision relies on me being demanding and Him being unreliable.

But if we hear this through the sounds of orality, we can hear something different. This isn't just a stranger who has come to my door at midnight, it's a friend. The friend has come to me on his journey because he knows that I'll shelter and feed him, no matter the time of day. Because he's my friend, I have an obligation to share what I have to help him. I go to you, my friend, because you have a similar obligation to me. What's yours is mine whenever I have need of it. When you give me weak excuses for not wanting to get out of bed, I keep banging on the door with my request.

What allows me to be a giant pain is that I'm also committed to helping you work out the good in your life, and letting you get away with poor excuses would be to fail you. I persist because in doing so, I exercise that third element of friendship. I'm demanding that you get up and give me your best. I'm demanding that you be your best by helping me fulfill my commitment to my other friend. I'm challenging you to live up to your commitment, even though the challenge might irritate you, because it's what is best for you. And the audacity that I show is that I'll keep after you until you do what you promised—not in spite of our friendship, but in the service of our friendship. You'll thank me in the morning. Heard this way, the story becomes a lesson in how great a privilege we have in approaching the Father in confidence, not how hard we need to work to get Him to care.

But Jesus doesn't leave us there: His challenge goes beyond how we could fail each other as friends. He tells us that if we ask Him, He will give; if we seek Him, we'll find, and if we knock, it will be opened. Not because we're demanding in the face of refusal, but because He wants us to be audacious in our belief that we can come to Him for whatever we need. And unlike the friend who gives us excuses until our persistence breaks through, He will never make excuses. His commitment to our friendship is greater than any human friend could ever fulfill. To an oral listener, Jesus is pitting His friendship against that of another person and showing us that His friendship is far greater.

The audacity and persistence that this shows isn't because I have a need and God is lazy, or because He's playing games with me to get me to realize just how much I want something. He's not teaching me lessons by depriving me of what I need. And in this story, I do have an obligation. The person who came to me is a friend, and I have a commitment to help them with whatever they need. And they're hungry, tired, and need shelter.

One common way that this passage gets preached is that it's our persistence in the face of God's reluctance that causes us to get what we need. We're told that the "eth" ending on *asketh, knocketh*, and *receiveth* means that we aren't supposed to ask just once. We're supposed to ask and then keep on asking until we receive. But this sounds like the story of the unjust judge (Luke 18:1–8), who is eventually persuaded to enact justice, not because he is committed to upholding justice, but because he's worn down by the woman's repeated petition. Are we ascribing to Jesus the same self-interest as Jesus describes in the judge? I hope not!

This lesson also raises an important question: If Jesus is to us like the homeowner, and our persistence is what finally gets Him to arise and give us what we ask for, how do we know when what we're asking for is good? If it's possible (even desirable) to overcome His reluctance by our repeated request, how do we know that we're not turning a *no* into a *yes* to our own harm?

We've all heard that God sometimes thinks our ideas aren't as good as His. We've all heard that we need to be careful that we don't insist on our own way until God relents and gives us what is bad for us. We've all heard that God gives us what we need until our stubbornness causes Him to give us what we want. But hearing the point of this story as *our persistence* can leave us unclear about how we know when a negative answer is the best answer.

And how about the reasons given by the homeowner for why he doesn't want to get up and give his friend what he needs? "I'm in bed, my kids are in bed, and I don't want to open the door." Please pardon me for being crude, but would that same excuse be acceptable if the homeowner needed to go to the bathroom during the night? I can't get up because the door is shut? And if it would be okay to get up to relieve yourself during the night, but too much to get up and give me bread, what kind of a friend are you being?

And we certainly don't want to ascribe that kind of reasoning to the Creator! "Sorry, I know you have a need, but I can't be bothered until you ask a whole bunch of times. I need to know that you really mean it.

You need to ask for bread more than once." In a culture where we are told to feed even our enemies, how much more is it our responsibility to feed our friends when they have a need?

So let's just go a little further: Jesus calls Himself the Bread of Life. Whoever eats that bread will not be hungry again. Bread is used over and over in stories and parables to represent life-sustaining nourishment. The disciples are told to feed His sheep. Now I'm hearing you say that when I ask you for bread to feed someone else who doesn't know you, I have to bang on your door and be a nuisance until you stop giving me lame excuses and share what you have?

Or would I hear the echo of Proverbs, which tells me that in times of trouble, I should go to my friend and my father's friend instead of my brother, because I have a greater claim on a friend than on my own family (27:10)? Or that one who has unreliable friends soon comes to ruin, but there is a friend who sticks closer than a brother? And that a friend loves at all times? And what of the stories told again and again of Abraham, the friend of God? Is this how God was to him? My suggestion is that a claim to friendship would be heard as a retelling of every story of friendship that I've heard since my youth. Does what I'm hearing resonate with how God has shown Himself to those who He has called "friend" in the past?

One could dismiss these questions by saying I'm taking the verse out of context. But keep in mind that for an oral thinker, there is no such thing as context. "Text and context" is an idea that depends on the primacy of writing to make sense. Text is the written verse that's being examined, and the context is the surrounding text. The comparison of text against context has been widened to mean text against historical and cultural elements, which are arrived at through the study of other written documents.

Text/context is a comparison of one written text with another, and to an oral thinker, there is no text/context comparison. There is only the memory of stories and wisdom sayings repeated over and over, until they become the fabric of thought itself. So yes, they are taken out of context, if by context we mean that what the gospel writer wrote down as being said by Jesus, compared to other written texts. But an oral culture has no such idea; they can only compare one story against the memory of other stories and listen for resonance.

It's become a staple of commentary and sermons to remark on Jesus' use of parables and stories rather than lectures to share His message. We'll suggest that He used stories because, as we're only now starting to realize, people retain more and listen more closely to stories than they do to lectures. How smart must He have been to have understood this centuries before psychologists understood it! And then we tell each other that we can learn from this, and instead of lecturing, we should tell stories.

I heard a radio announcer say this while I was driving to my office this morning, and the absurdity struck me as it always does. Jesus didn't use the lecture or sermon format because it hadn't been invented yet. No one in antiquity lectured or structured their lessons in modern literary form. The biggest reason we have a hard time reading ancient philosophers is that they aren't written like modern lectures. They're dialogues between two or more people, where several points of view are discussed and hashed out. They never seem to come to the point until every participant has had their say. To the modern mind, that's like watching paint dry! When less than 3 percent of your audience can write their name, and where orality is the only way to share knowledge with them, is there any other choice?

What we know as the academic lecture, or sermon, is an invention of literacy. It's a form that makes information captured in written form easy to deliver and test, but impossible to remember. The idea that a sermon starts with a text, gives us three main points, two illustrations, a couple of quotes from some dead white guy with a strange beard, and ends with an appeal to emotions, is nowhere to be found in antiquity.

It's a creation of the eighteenth-century Enlightenment, made possible by the shift from orality to primary literacy.

In short, the biggest reason that Jesus didn't use modern sermon form to teach is that it hadn't been invented yet. The predominant form of teaching was oral, through dialogue and disputation, for several centuries, and the epistles followed those forms as oral creations spoken to companions who captured them. The religious world had parable, prophetic proclamation, and compilations of sayings written down and shared by followers. The Q document is a good example.

That's a difficult thought to grasp, but oral thinkers identify what they hear through similarity. Jesus uttered the phrase "He that hath ears to hear, let him hear (Matthew 11:12)" frequently to bear witness to the truth of what He was saying. He often used it to reinforce parables, which had no clear didactic meaning, but to attest to the truthfulness of what was heard. "My sheep hear my voice; they won't hear another, and nothing will pluck them out of my hand. They may be fooled by what they see, but never by what they hear, because the sound of my voice is unmistakable. In fact, the evil and adulterous generation seeks a sign (a visual cue), which causes them to be led astray." And at the Mount of Transfiguration, the voice that spoke from the heavens told the disciples to *listen* to Jesus, not to erect monuments to their experience.

Sound Pattern Recognition

If you've ever spent much time around musicians, you can get a sense of how sound pattern recognition can work. When our children were small, we'd sing lots of songs: Sunday school songs, learning songs from school, and kids' TV songs. They made a big impression. Thirty years after *Blue's Clues*, I have to stop myself from wailing when I go outside to check the mail. It's amazing how many common phrases have been used as parts of popular songs, and one of the games would be to pick up on something the other person said, and start singing a popular song that used the phrase. Musicians often do this, and it can be really frustrating if you don't know what's happening. You say "that'll be the day" and they immediately start singing the song. Or you say "I wonder" and they start to sing about the book of love. Say "tell me why" and before you finish the sentence, they're singing a Beatles tune. Or just say the word "help" and you hear another Beatles tune. Just yesterday morning (sorry, James Taylor), I heard someone say "watch me" and we all nae-naed.

Sound pattern recognition can also connect thoughts through jumps from sound to sound. I can hear a phrase of the "Hallelujah Chorus" from Handel's *Messiah*, jump from that to "Yes, We Have No Bananas," and end up at "Camptown Races" within the chorus. Or witness the popularity of YouTube videos where musicians play twenty popular tunes in four minutes because they all use the same chord progression. Hearing one can trigger the next, and so on, and those jumps aren't connected by logic.

I won't say that there is context, since *context* is a term that depends on a written text against which a snippet of writing can be compared back to the whole. Without writing, there can't be the dilemma of the hermeneutic circle. (When working with a text, you can't fully understand the whole until you can understand all of the parts, but you can't adequately describe all of the parts unless you know the whole.)

It's much like putting a puzzle together. You can't do it unless you can identify where the piece goes, but you can't identify the piece unless you're looking at the whole picture. But this doesn't apply to a piece of music, which is sound that dies away upon its hearing and where each part is heard at the same time. A world of sound isn't divisible into separate sounds in the way that modern recording equipment can make it.

How Far Does Friendship Go?

The hypothetical situation that Jesus presents to the disciples raises the question of how far the liberty and responsibility of being face-to-face can extend. If I'm truly a friend of Jesus, how far must I go to fulfill my obligations? And how much liberty do I have to stand face-to-face with Him? The story of Abraham gives us some clues.

Abraham has long been known as the friend of God. By now it should be clear that the Bible writers weren't referring to modern notions of friendship. Abraham wasn't called a friend because he had shared all of the details of his inner self with Jehovah. As we'll see, Abraham exercised all three elements of friendship in Genesis 18. The familiar story starts with Abraham sitting in his tent door, when he sees three figures approaching.

> And the LORD appeared unto him in the plains of Mamre: and he sat in the tent door in the heat of the day; And he lift up his eyes and looked, and, lo, three men stood by him: and when he saw *them*, he ran to meet them from the tent door, and bowed himself toward the ground, And said, My Lord, if now I have found favour in thy sight, pass not away, I pray thee, from thy servant: Let a little water, I pray you, be fetched, and wash your feet, and rest yourselves under the tree: And I will fetch a morsel of bread, and comfort ye your hearts; after that ye shall pass on: for therefore are ye come to your servant. And they said, So do, as thou hast said. (Genesis 18:1–5)

The next several moments describe Abraham's lengthy preparation of roasted kid and bread, which he sets before the men. After they've eaten, the conversation turns to Sarah and her inability to conceive, and a promise is made that next year at this same time, Sarah will have a child of her own. After Sarah laughs at the thought of an older woman with a baby, the Lord asks Abraham if anything is too hard for the Lord. Then the men rise up to continue on their journey.

And the men rose up from thence, and looked toward Sodom: and Abraham went with them to bring them on the way. And the LORD said, Shall I hide from Abraham that thing which I do; Seeing that Abraham shall surely become a great and mighty nation, and all the nations of the earth shall be blessed in him? For I know him, that he will command his children and his household after him, and they shall keep the way of the LORD, to do justice and judgment; that the LORD may bring upon Abraham that which he hath spoken of him. And the LORD said, Because the cry of Sodom and Gomorrah is great, and because their sin is very grievous; I will go down now, and see whether they have done altogether according to the cry of it, which is come unto me; and if not, I will know.

And the men turned their faces from thence, and went toward Sodom: but Abraham stood yet before the LORD. And Abraham drew near, and said, Wilt thou also destroy the righteous with the wicked? Peradventure there be fifty righteous within the city: wilt thou also destroy and not spare the place for the fifty righteous that are therein? That be far from thee to do after this manner, to slay the righteous with the wicked: and that the righteous should be as the wicked, that be far from thee: Shall not the Judge of all the earth do right? And the LORD said, If I find in Sodom fifty righteous within the city, then I will spare all the place for their sakes. (vv. 16–26)

Then follows the familiar exchange where Abraham starts bargaining God down to smaller and smaller numbers—from fifty to forty-five, then forty, then thirty, then twenty, and finally ten, each time apologizing for his audacity in even speaking to the Lord. And each time the Lord relents and goes lower, based on the premise that Abraham has declared—that it's not just for the righteous to be destroyed along with the wicked. There are echoes of orality in this exchange that get lost in later translations, which are made for increasingly literate readers. One of the main reasons for using the King James isn't because it's better than others, but because it was translated prior to widespread literacy, so it retains much more of an oral resonance than later translations.

For example, the endless embellishment of simple actions, such as "and he lifted up his eyes and looked, and lo, three men stood by him: and when he saw them, he ran," seems redundant to a modern eye. But to an oral ear, repetition establishes rhythm, sets the stage, and gives time for the hearer to create the mental picture of the event.

This repetition, which the Greeks called *copia*, is characteristic of the Old Testament more than the New, and of the Gospels more than the later epistles. While it seems like it may just be a matter of style, it's also a storyteller's technique of layering detail into the story to convey a point. One of the reasons we do new translations is because the old versions seem strange to our literate eyes, and the very things that are written out are the elements of sound. And it's it some of the small details that we can hear the faint echoes of the obligations and privileges of friendship.

To begin with, Abraham clearly recognizes who he's speaking with from the beginning of the story. He sees them from a distance, recognizes the Lord, and runs to them, bowing down as he arrives. An astute ear might hear this as the reverse of the actions in the story of the prodigal, where the father recognizes the son and runs to him while the son is yet a long way off. Once Abraham arrives in front of them (and stands in the way of their journey), he entreats them to stop, eat, and rest.

Then he says something extremely important: "Comfort ye your hearts. After that ye shall pass on: for therefore are you come to your servant" (v. 5). Abraham knows who this is, and recognizes the Lord's distress over what he's about to do. Abraham doesn't ask; he *declares* that the Lord has come to him to seek the comfort of a friend: "Your heart is troubled; stop, eat, rest, and find comfort. That's why you're here."

As a trusted friend, Abraham has already gotten in the Lord's face, and offered food, rest, and companionship to comfort his friend. At this point, a modern preacher might pause and point out that the reason Abraham could recognize the Lord at a distance was because he was sitting in his tent door, during the hottest part of the day, and looking outward rather than looking at his phone. He was taking time to rest and look around him at the world, not thinking about anything, and was able to see opportunity before it passed him by. He wasn't distracted by putting it in the chat!

Once Abraham recognizes his friend, he doesn't just walk to meet him. Abraham runs. He rejoices to see his friend, and clearly takes pleasure in being with him. He offers him water to wash his feet, and invites him to dine and rest. He offers all he has for his friend's comfort, and goes to great effort to prepare a simple meal. Abraham selects his best kid, and causes it to be butchered and roasted, while he prepares and bakes fresh bread. This takes hours, and I sometimes wonder if Abraham is stalling the Lord because he knows what the Lord is on his way to do. There aren't too many things that the Lord could be distressed over, and Abraham is pretty well acquainted with the reputation of the city where his nephew Lot and his family live.

But it's after the meal, and the discussion about how God plans to fulfill His promise to make a great and mighty nation out of Abraham, that we see the full extent of friendship. The three men get up to go on their way, and two of them turn toward the direction they were going at the beginning of the story. But the Lord stops and says, "Shall I hide from Abraham that thing which I do?" (v. 17). Notice that He doesn't just think it; He *says it.* He gives voice to the question. And He speaks the reason why He feels compelled to tell Abraham where He's going:

"For I know him, that he will command his children and his household after him, and they shall keep the way of the LORD, to do justice and judgment" (v. 19).

Think of what the Lord has just spoken: "I know him. I know what he will do. And I know that he will exemplify justice and judgment, and shall keep the way of the Lord." He's answered the question that Abraham asked at the beginning when he asked if the Lord had come to him because He was distressed. The answer is yes: "I've come to you because I know exactly what you will do." And it's at the moment that the men start toward Sodom that Abraham does what seems the most audacious thing possible: He gets in God's face. Abraham stops God physically by blocking His path. He stood before the Lord, face-to-face, and began to plead for the lives of the people of Sodom.

Listen to the appeals that Abraham makes as he pleads with His friend. "What if there are righteous people there? Is it right to destroy them along with the wicked? Would you spare the city for the sake of fifty righteous?" And then Abraham offers the argument that the Lord has just given him when He described Abraham: adherence to justice and judgment. "That be far from thee to do after this manner, to slay the righteous with the wicked: and that the righteous should be as the wicked, that be far from thee: Shall not the Judge of all the earth do right?" (v. 25).

This is not just an appeal to what is right and just; it is slicing to the heart of the Lord's dilemma. "Stop," he says. "This is not your best. This would not be right! This is not what you, the Judge of all the earth, do." Over and over, Abraham apologizes for his audacity as he reduces the number from fifty to ten, and his apology is not just a device; it's because he knows the risk involved in what he's doing. "Lord, please be patient with me; for I am but dust" is how Abraham begins each of his moves.

There's a lot that we can learn from the story, but an oral thinker would hear how far Abraham was willing to go to fulfill his friendship.

He's willing to risk all to stand before the Lord, face-to-face, and do what's necessary to help Him work out wisdom, justice, and mercy. And it's pretty clear that the Lord isn't surprised by Abraham's actions. The two statements linger long after the story ends: "I know why you've come to me," and "I know exactly what you will do." As true friends, Abraham has stood before the Lord to turn justice into mercy, while the Lord has sought Abraham to help Him spare Lot. Even though the Lord carries out His justice, He still leans on His friend once more. He phones a friend!

This is a heavy burden. A friend must be willing to risk it all to demand that their friend rise to their best. This isn't focused in any way on me, for the risk is not that you'd reject me; the risk is that you'd accept my offer and obligate me to carry through. And this is why we're told that friendship with the world is enmity with God. Many have struggled with the apparent contradiction that we must be in the world but not be friends with the world. From a modern, literate stance that sees friendship as information exchange and disclosure, we have friends at all levels, and all relationships work the same way.

For the oral thinker, friendship is a special relationship that entails commitment and risk of all one has in the service of the other person. To be friends with the world is enmity with God, because one cannot pledge all that they have to what the world represents, the fruit of disobedience to God. The world represents the desire to hide from God, and to do it in our own strength. We simply can't commit all that we have to helping the world fulfill that goal.

Imagine the courage it took to stand before the Creator and Judge, and remind Him of what is right and wrong. Imagine the terror Abraham must have felt as he pleaded for mercy for the city, all the while pleading for the Lord's patience and kindness to prevail. Had the Lord forgotten justice? Had He, in His anger, forgotten His own mercy? Or had He come to Abraham because He knew Abraham would do what the angels could not, which was to stand face-to-face with Him as a friend and call Him to what was right?

Abraham could do this because he understood that a friend must be willing to risk his own safety in the service of his friend. I believe that the Lord went to Abraham so that Abraham could stand face-to-face with God and challenge Him to let mercy prevail.

As we hear echoed in James, mercy is as much part of God's character as justice and judgment, but Abraham calls on God to let mercy prevail: "For he shall have judgment without mercy, that hath showed no mercy; and mercy rejoiceth against judgment" (James 2:13). Mercy stands face-to-face with judgment, and mercy wins the life of Lot and his family. Just as Jacob would later stand face-to-face with the angel and say, "I have seen God face to face, and my life is preserved" (Genesis 32:30). Abraham stands face-to-face with His Creator.

I've heard more than one preacher say that they wondered what it would be like for the Creator and Redeemer to talk with us as He did with Abraham. What if the Lord said, "I'm about to go do something in the earth, but I'm just not going to do it without checking in with my friend first. I know what they'll do. They'll pray for whatever I'm about to do." This is the perfect picture of intercession—of us praying for a situation or person because God has prompted us to do it.

But what if we understood that it's more than just knowing something, and more than just an infrequent task that needs to be done? What if we understood that every time the Lord seeks and prompts us to pray about a situation, He's inviting us to fulfill the bonds of friendship with Him? And what if we understood that every act of obedience in His plan is more than just slavish work on our part; it's us entering into a moment when we can stand face-to-face with Him, and help Him accomplish His best in the world He's created? And finally, what if we understood the amazing privilege we have to stand face-to-face with Him?

Until Jesus came on the scene, this is a privilege that few had. Besides Abraham and Jacob, few have been able to stand before God this way.

Moses tells Israel that this is what God seeks for all of His people, and even suggests that they could have done so if they'd had the courage to trust God. At the moment when he delivers the Ten Commandments, he begins by proclaiming:

> Hear, O Israel, the statutes and judgments which I speak in your ears this day, that ye may learn them, and keep, and do them. The LORD our God made a covenant with us in Horeb. The LORD made not this covenant with our fathers, but with us, *even* us, who *are* all of us here alive this day. The LORD talked with you face to face in the mount out of the midst of the fire. (Genesis 5:1–4)

Or think of Gideon in Judges 6:22, who says, when he realizes who he's been talking to, "Alas, Sovereign LORD! I have seen the angel of the LORD face to face!" It's the presumption of equality that is both terrifying and encouraging to these oral thinkers. It's the same thought that energizes Paul's comment to the Corinthians, "for now we see through a glass darkly: but then face to face: now I know if part; but then shall I know even as also I am known" (1 Corinthians 13:12). When I stand face-to-face with Him, I will know Him as well as He knows me. But for Paul, there's no terror. There's only love and complete joy, and it's a love that can be found by all who seek the Lord.

The Limits of Friendship

These are the commitments of friendship in an oral culture: "I take pleasure in your company, what's mine is yours, and I commit everything I have now and in the future to helping you work out the highest and best you can be. I pledge myself to your benefit." Modern friendship is a reversal of these, because of the focus on self and the fact that the friendship always carries within itself the seeds of its own demise. We may formalize our relationship by contract, whether partner or by marriage, but this only slows down the parting. We are taught to go into relationships looking for our own benefit. And finally, we are taught to regard communication as self-serving, benefiting the other person only after we have expressed ourselves. In short, adopting modern views of communication pushes us further away from each other and from God.

How far does friendship take us? How far did Jesus go to demonstrate true friendship? One of the most searing moments of Jesus' last week in bodily form was in the Garden of Gethsemane. At the last supper, Jesus spoke of His coming betrayal:

> Now when the even was come, he sat down with the twelve. And as they did eat, he said, Verily I say unto you, that one of you shall betray me. And they were exceeding sorrowful, and began every one of them to say unto him, Lord, is it I? And he answered and said, He that dippeth *his* hand with me in the dish, the same shall betray me. The Son of man goeth as it is written of him: but woe unto that man by whom the Son of man is betrayed! it had been good for that man if he had not been born. Then Judas, which betrayed him, answered and said, Master, is it I? He said unto him, Thou hast said. (Matthew 26:20–25)

Later that evening, Jesus takes Peter and the sons of Zebedee, his closest disciples, and prays in the garden, and as He finishes, Judas comes with a crowd to arrest Jesus:

> Now he that betrayed him gave them a sign, saying, Whomsoever I shall kiss, that same is he: hold him fast. And forthwith he came to Jesus, and said, Hail, master; and kissed him. And Jesus said unto him, Friend, where-

> fore art thou come? Then came they, and laid hands on
> Jesus, and took him. (vv. 48–50)

Other translations render Jesus' reaction as "Friend, do what you came for." Instead of a question, it's a statement. Notice that Judas calls Jesus master, but Jesus responds by calling Judas friend? Think of what Jesus is offering here by calling Judas friend, knowing what Judas has done. "In spite of your betrayal, in spite of the fact that you cared more about your own comfort than my very life, in spite of the fact that you and I both knew you were going to do this, my offer still stands. I still take pleasure in your company, what's mine is still yours, and I'm still willing to help you grow in wisdom and understanding. No matter what you've done, I'm still offering you friendship!" It's significant that Judas can't bring himself to call Jesus friend; instead, he calls Him master. Just plain teacher. Not friend.

To catch how amazing this is, Jesus has already told Judas that He knows what's going to happen and what Judas has done. Throughout the week, He's been talking with His followers about His coming betrayal and death. At supper, He tells the disciples that one of them will betray Him. Then He hands Judas a piece of bread and says that the one He gives the bread to is the one who will betray Him. Judas asks if it's him, and Jesus just says, "You've said it."

Think of how this would sound, after repeatedly saying, "One of you will betray me." Judas finally speaks it, and Jesus confirms it. But these aren't accusations; these are opportunities for Judas to tell Jesus what he's done. The warnings that Jesus gives aren't going to change what's going to happen; they're opportunities for Judas to apologize and be forgiven! Jesus is acting as a friend by giving Judas every opportunity to repent and be restored.

Jesus even tells Judas that His death is unavoidable, that it's prophesied and planned, and that nothing will change it. He also says that the person who betrays Him is in trouble, and that it would be better for that man not to have been born. This isn't condemnation; it's giving Judas a chance to repent. Jesus is telling Judas that He knows what's happening, that it has to happen, but that Judas can still be forgiven. Judas is fulfilling an important part of the plan of God, because it has to be a friend who betrays Jesus.

At the moment of betrayal, Jesus looks at Judas and addresses Him as *friend*. Even at that last moment, Judas could have repented and still carried through with his plan to identify Jesus for the crowd. Jesus' thoughts are not for Himself and whether He got His message across, but for His friend, for whom He is about to lay down His life.

We don't think well of Judas. We judge his sin of betrayal to be worse than any other sin. But Peter does the same thing when he denies knowing Jesus. Just like He does with Judas, Jesus gives Peter the chance to change his mind and his actions by telling him that He knows what Peter will do. Even at the last moment in the garden, He tells Peter that Peter will deny knowing Him three times before morning.

Both Peter and Judas are struck by their grief, and by the love Jesus has shown in treating them as true friends in His last moments together with them. But unlike Peter, Judas repents before the priests, who are unsympathetic to say the least. "That's your problem; you deal with it," they tell him when he tries to return the thirty pieces of silver. Torn by his grief, Judas goes out and hangs himself. Peter, too, is struck by grief and remorse, but he lives with it until he can face Jesus after the resurrection, and then he repents when he can stand face-to-face.

I don't know if Peter really believed that Jesus would return, but I think Peter believed that forgiveness was possible. I believe that he truly heard the message of forgiveness that Jesus spoke over and over, and was able to live in hope that Jesus really meant what He said. I also truly believe that Judas could have repented and lived, had he believed that Jesus really meant it.

There is much to be learned from the moment in the garden, and I don't want to take away from any of those truths. What I do want us to hear is the amazing offer of friendship that Jesus makes in His most trying moments. At His very worst, moments after He has prayed for the cup to pass from Him, moments after He has subjected Himself to the Father's will, and even while He is reconciling Himself with dying the worst possible death the Romans could devise, His thoughts turn to His friends. At the moment when He is faced with the worst, He still looks at His betrayer and offers all that He has to help his betrayer live.

When Jesus looks at Judas and asks, "Friend, wherefore art thou come?" ("Why are you here?"), He is offering forgiveness. Three simple words, "to betray you," would have been enough to rise to the offer of friendship that Jesus makes. And without consciously knowing it, Judas is acting as a friend by helping Jesus fulfill the prophesied destiny that He has just struggled to accept. The covenant of friendship made by Abraham was binding on succeeding generations, and Judas was still a son of Abraham.

Judas is helping Jesus fulfill the plan spoken through the ages, from the moment when Adam and Eve left the garden of Eden. Judas is fulfilling the promise of friendship made by Abraham, by Moses, by Gideon, by Elijah, and by all of those who have stood face-to-face as friends with God through the ages. That promise is to help their friend carry out their best, and at the moment of betrayal, Judas could have asked, like Abraham, "Isn't that why you've come to your friend?"

Three Words for Love

Anyone who has followed Christ for any length of time knows that there are three words for love in the ancient Greek language: *agape, eros,* and *phileo*. Eros refers to the physical, sensual, embodied appetites of humanity; phileo refers to friendship; and agape refers to love that is seen in selfless giving, which is epitomized by Jesus' sacrifice for us.

The problem with this understanding, which has become a common-place of interpreting Paul's letters, is that it wasn't written until centuries after Paul used the terms in his letters. But is this what a first-century, oral thinker would have heard? That there are only three ways to define the word *love*, and that agape is the highest form of love? Let's just imag-ine for a moment that we're living in Athens, where Paul introduces the idea of Jesus to the philosophers in the marketplace.

These are the thought leaders of the day, the guys who would have been all over the Sunday morning talk shows. They have no clue who Jesus is, and have never heard of His ministry off in some obscure, dusty corner of the world. Would they have nodded and said, "Yup, that nails it. When we think of agape, we think of God's incarnation and sacrifice on our behalf," or would they have said something else? They have been using the word and exploring the concept in their philosophies for centuries. The philosophers who make up Paul's audience have a tradition and his-tory for concepts like love, and it's into that rich tradition that Paul speaks.

We modern literates think of the word eros as referring primarily to the sexual appetites, and in our modern dualism, we tend to equate eros with sin. It's the part of us that is dangerous and leads us astray. This is an echo of dualism, which saw everything physical as inferior and there-fore of no value. But to the oral thinkers of the day, eros was much more. It went beyond just the sexual urges, to become, as one modern philos-opher writes, "the driving force that lies behind every human creation and that sustains every human act of greatness and strength and power."*

It's love that seeks to bring forth good things, and that is seen in taking control. In its proper exercise between too much and too little, eros is the motivation to create, to bring order to chaos, and to sustain life itself. As with the other virtues, one could exercise too much or too little within the laws and customs of the community. But a mature person would seek to exercise the correct balance between too much and too little for the

---

*   Carl G, Vaught, "Two Meditations on Love." *Drew Gateway* 53, no. 1 (Fall 1982): 35

circumstances. Thus, if I went to work to provide for my family and did it well, that would be motivated by eros. I could do too little work and be regarded as lazy, and I could do too much work and be regarded as greedy, and either of those extremes would be unwise. But the practical wise person would understand and display the right balance between too much and too little.

The second word we translate as the highest form of love is agape. This word focuses not on what a person needs or desires, but on what a person gives away, even when there seems to be no reason for it. The word was the most profound expression that could be used to characterize a gratuitous act. Jesus uses this term when He asks Peter if he loves Him: "Simon, lovest thou me?" (John 21:17). Do you love me in a manner that would make you respond to me without expecting anything in return? It's love that is seen in giving away, and it too can be exercised too much or too little. I could give away all that I had, to my own harm, and be thought unwise. On the other hand, I could share too little and be thought ungenerous. Either extreme would be unwise.

The third term, which we have relegated to secondary status, is philia. Literate thinkers look at philia as inferior to agape, which is seen in God's expression of love for us. We reduce philia to mean friendship on a human level, because we read it through the modern, therapeutic model of self-disclosure, reciprocal exchange of hidden information, and self-validation. You're just my buddy because I've told you my secrets, and that's fine, but God's love goes way beyond that to care for me. However, in the ancient Greek tradition, philia is much more than that. Listen to philosopher Carl Vaught:

> Finally, though, there is a third word for love, and in my judgment, this word is the highest of all—the word philia. Philia is not the kind of love that lacks something and wants to be fulfilled, nor is it the kind of love that simply gives itself away, gratuitously. Rather, it points to

the communion between one person and another where there is no longer any question of wanting, or giving, or receiving. In this case, the communion has become so intimate that wanting and receiving have been transcended altogether. It is this word that Jesus uses when he describes his relationship with His own Father. God loves (phileo) the son in that intimate kind of way that has already transcended the question of giving and receiving.*

When Jesus appears to the disciples after His resurrection, He asks Peter if Peter loves Him. He begins by asking, "Peter, do you love [agape] me?" Peter responds, "Yes, Lord, you know that I love you [phileo]." We see this as Jesus asking if Peter loves Him with the highest form (agape) and Peter not being able to make the same commitment back to Jesus. The question comes a second time, in the same formulation. Then the third time, Jesus asks if Peter loves Him (phileo) and Peter responds that he loves (phileo) Jesus. "Then feed my sheep," Jesus says.

We read this as Jesus beginning with the highest form of love, but then backing down on the commitment to love in a sacrificial way, to meet Peter's inability to bring himself to that original level of love.

But in the oral tradition, Jesus has begun with the lesser love, and Peter responds with the greater. The third time, Jesus escalates the question from "Do you love me enough to give yourself gratuitously, for no reason, if I ask?" to "Do you love me with a love that goes beyond the acts of giving and receiving to simply being with me in a bond of mutual affection?" In other words, "Can your love for me transcend busyness to being? Can you be one with me, and can your actions come out of that love rather than being a way to try to win my love? Can you stand face-to-face with me? If so, then the best way to show it is to take care

---

*   Vaught, "Two Meditations," 35

of what I most care about while I'm gone. Help me accomplish my plan, by teaching those who haven't met me about my love."[*]

Friendship and Deep Secrets

In 2011, therapist and researcher Niobe Way wrote a book about boys' friendships in the modern world. Way was struck by the lack of attention given by psychologists to the role of friendship among young pre-adolescent males. What little attention was given in the literature assumed that boys found it difficult to make friends. Her work was written after twenty years of working with inner-city boys as they dealt with depression, substance addiction, gang behavior, and suicide.

Contrary to the prevailing view that boys couldn't make friends, Way found that younger boys instinctively developed close friendships that they described in terms very similar to the elements of the classical model. Trust, interdependence, respect, equality, focus on the other person above oneself, and commitment to the other's welfare characterized these close relationships.

But Way also traced how these pre-adolescent males are forced to abandon their friendships around age fourteen, at which point their other behavior changed remarkably. Delinquency, depression, drug use, crime, death by violence, and suicide increased dramatically once they abandoned those friendships. The correlation was so strong that success in later years could be predicted by whether those early friendships were maintained or lost.

The young men attributed the abandonment of friendship as a necessary part of growing up and leaving their childhood. Way, however, explores how formal and informal teaching about how relationships *should* work forces them to abandon relationships that have nurtured and sustained them to this point. She traces the root cause back to homophobia—the fear

---

[*]   Vaught, 35.

that a close relationship that includes feelings of affection beyond those for casual friends would be evidence of same-sex attraction.

In other words, Way finds that young boys are able to form and nurture life-sustaining friendships until they are taught that such friendships are wrong, at which point they substitute the modern understanding of friendship. In part, Way is showing us that our modern notions of friendship result in relationships that don't bring life, and cause us to abandon true friendships to our own personal and societal harm. She goes well beyond an objective study to advocacy, pleading with us to understand that teaching our youth to abandon true friendship is killing our kids.*

Way published her study in 2011, before the most recent redefining of the word *friend* to mean a count of how many people read your tweets. And while Way was studying a smaller population, and could trace cause and effect much more closely, I'd suggest that we can see the same trend in our youth today on a broader scale. Facebook friendships are thinner than even modern notions of friendship involving reciprocal exchange, as they are based on one-way information flow only. I tweet my thoughts, you like them, so you follow. There's little to no reciprocity, only a demand for more and more revelation of personal information to the reader. Perhaps the erosion of civility and the rise of intolerance of other people's faults mirrors the loss of even a thin form of friendship, with the same results on a broader societal scale.

I also believe that Way's work shows us a simple yet profound truth. We are intuitively drawn to make true friendships, until we are taught that those friendships are wrong. As oral beings with a veneer of literacy, we are predisposed to form life-sustaining friendships, until we are taught by adults that we must leave those friendships behind. As children, who are predominantly oral until they are taught to be literate thinkers, we are able to live in the kinds of friendships that Jesus offers

---

*   Niobe Way, *Deep Secrets: Boys Friendships and the Crisis of Connection.* (Cambridge: Harvard University Press, 2011),

to us, until we grow up and learn otherwise. The move from oral to literate thought involves cutting oneself off from what sustains emotional life in favor of information exchange leading to self-validation.

It's as if we are left naked and ashamed when our eyes are opened by the knowledge of good and evil. It's interesting that other scholars trace differences in thinking about friendships between modern highly literate cultures and highly oral cultures, and find that modern-day oral cultures place a much greater emphasis on friendship as an outward commitment than a tool for self-validation.

In 1974, the US Supreme Court made a decision that changed the landscape of education. The court held that the State of Wisconsin could not place Amish children under compulsory education past the eighth grade. The state argued that public interest demanded that children be in school until the tenth grade, while the court found that no public purpose could be served by forcing an additional two years of education in the face of a long-standing religious tradition and belief.

The court found that the children had gained the tools of literacy sufficient to function in modern society by the eighth grade, and an additional two years of learning wouldn't produce a benefit great enough to warrant violating the right to free exercise of religion. The decision has been the foundation of a parent's right to educate privately. It's been used numerous times since then to undergird parents' rights to send children to religious schools, and to support homeschooling efforts.

What I find fascinating, for our journey, is why the lawyers for the Amish argued that compulsory education past the eighth grade was detrimental to their community and a threat to their very existence. It didn't come out of convenience, as the young men were just as capable of working on the farm at fourteen as they were at sixteen. Their argument came from a long-standing practice of avoiding anything in the modern world that would encourage the person to see themselves as separate from the community.

As John Hostettler explains, much of Amish life revolves around maintaining group identity over self-identity. Many of the customs of clothing, transportation, housing, and other outward elements are carefully controlled to show no difference. Hostettler tells us that this is because the Amish believe that modern notions of individuality are corrosive to the community. Seeing the self as separate from, and different than, the rest of the group leads to comparison, judgment, status differences, and the ultimate destruction of the community.*

In their uneasy encounters with the modern world, in which every outward element of life is seen as a message about the self and its own validation, the Amish believed that teaching about science was the most corrosive. The scientific method involves defining the whole, then defining and separating the elements that make up the whole, followed by testable hypotheses regarding the inner workings of cause and effect between the elements. Amish leaders believed that teaching the children to see themselves and everything in life in atomistic and reductionist terms teaches them to despise their tradition.

In other words, scientific literacy is useful to a certain point, but beyond that, it becomes a destructive force in the community. Thus, a horse and carriage is a necessary tool, and the science and engineering that goes into designing and building a buggy is good. But nothing about the exterior of the buggy should suggest that the owner is an individual who is better than or worse than any other buggy driver. It's the comparative part of the thought process that threatens—the tendency to reduce things to separate elements and compare them against the whole.

It's striking that the Amish saw the point at which modern teaching becomes corrosive to their community to be the same age when the young boys in Way's experience destroy their friendships. It's the same age when we start teaching modern theories about relationships—how they're formed, what they're for, and how they're sustained.

---

*   John Hostetler, *Amish Society* (Baltimore: Johns Hopkins University Press, 1993.

I was driving recently and listening to an expert on marriage on a national syndicated Christian station. In his thirty-second slice of profundity, the expert on marriage relationships made the statement that men who don't abandon male friendships when they get married are violating God's plan. What a horrible thing to teach—that we should isolate ourselves from anyone other than our spouse, in a relationship built on mechanistically driven information exchange, or worse, on a series of self-validating "likes."

If we are fortunate enough to have a friend who is willing to stand by and help us when we need help, and be willing to make available whatever they have available for my good, we should be thankful! But instead, we teach isolation and the rejection of real friendships, formed before our eyes are opened by our teachers, in favor of empty relationships that have our self as the beginning and ending. Now throw in social media, which reduces communication to messages sent and approval gained, ramps up the risk of censure for placing a foot wrong, and leaves us emptier than before.

In a recent church service I attended, the worship leader kept saying that God wants a relationship with us, not religion. And I had to wonder, *What kind of relationship are you encouraging me to have? The kind we've been taught to form, or the kind that Jesus offers to us?* Jesus told us that He didn't call us servants, He called us friends. And when He did, He wasn't saying that He liked our latest social media post. He was saying that He enjoyed our company, that what was His was ours, and that He was committing everything that He had to help us grow and mature. He was offering to treat us like a king would treat another sovereign—as an equal, standing face-to-face in mutual respect and strength.

And He showed us what that really means, by demonstrating the extent to which a friend will go in the service of His friends: "Greater love hath no man than this, that a man lay down his life for his friends" (John 15:13). A friend will persist long after others have gone away, not because of desperation but because a friend won't let their friend get away with less than their best. A friend will persist in offering forgiveness, as Jesus gave Judas numerous opportunities to change his mind and be restored.

Instead, we teach that relationships are built on information exchange, with self-disclosure as the coin of the realm. But Shannon is about information transfer—content only—and about me getting my way. It's not about human growth but about power, the ability to be understood and agreed with by you. Even though later thinkers have created all sorts of secondary terms to include elements like non-verbal and mediated channels, the models still assume that shared understanding comes out of the receiver understanding the intention of the speaker who starts it all.

While it's good that the models have evolved, they can be no better than the underlying assumptions. It would be like putting fuzzy dice on the mirror of a nuclear submarine. We teach that marriages are modeled on intimacy, which is measured by the kind and amount of information exchanged. In that model are the conditions and justifications for ending the relationship, when you stop disclosing, when you withdraw, or when I judge that what I'm getting out of it isn't enough to warrant the risk.

In other words, modern teaching about relationships has little to do with what an oral thinker would have heard, and very little to do with what Jesus modeled as the highest relationship He could offer! If we've been fortunate enough to have developed friendships, we're taught that they must be abandoned when we grow up and put away childish things. In short, we have no real friendships; our marriages are stressed, and we are alone, ashamed of the real friendships that we do have.

What if we were to model our teaching about marriage on the elements of friendship in an oral world? What if we saw deep emotional attachment coming out of the commitments that Jesus modeled before us? What if we committed ourselves by saying, "I take pleasure in your company. All that I have is yours. I'm committing everything I have to helping you work out balance, moderation, and practical wisdom? Whatever it takes for you to find and grow in the purposes of God, to the full extent of His plan for you and me together?"

That kind of friendship persists in calling the other to grow, regardless of the cost. That kind of friendship stands in the street, pounding on the door if necessary, because I won't let you take the easy way out. That kind of friendship forgives, but like Jesus and Judas, doesn't excuse or ignore. That kind of friendship believes all things, hopes all things, endures all things, and never fails. That kind of friendship doesn't happen *because* we are genuine and honest; it *allows* us to be genuine and honest because we won't be rejected.

When the doctor discovers cancer, that kind of commitment carries both through the storm. In the face of possible death, that kind of commitment allows for the acceptance of possible loss, and helps make death the culmination of a joint commitment. When my wife had a bout with lymphoma, we had to pray through the issue of loss, and I had the chance to live out the hypothetical question I'd discussed with pre-seminary students many times. How would you counsel someone who was faced with the possible loss of a spouse or loved one? And would you rather face it yourself or have your spouse face it?

As I'd shared with the students, when my wife and I made our vows, they included sickness and health, and richer or poorer, till death do us part. Our wedding vows contained the certainty that one of us would die before the other. But we also believed that what came after death was the whole point of living. In fact, death was an appointment, not a tragedy. It would be the Lord bringing us home, and while either of us would grieve the loss, we would be able to celebrate that the purpose of our friendship was fulfilled.

Given the choice, I'd rather face the loss so my closest friend doesn't have to face it. I'd rather experience the sorrow and heartache than let my friend go through it. I'd rather be home myself, but if God chooses for me to stay, I want it to be to help my friend make it. And while no loss is ever convenient or part of *my* plan, it is inescapable. Perhaps that's one reason so many marriages end in divorce, because terminating the relationship on our terms is easier than accepting God's ending. In my opinion, it's also why we feel compelled to turn every untimely death into an act of heroism, and every death into a failure of modern medicine.* Contrast this with Lazarus, Jesus' friend, who didn't complain at all when his first temporary death solidified Jesus' claim to be the resurrection and the life!

Sharing or Fixing?

I live in a part of the country where hunting, fishing, and boating are a way of life. The year seems to revolve around the four seasons: hunting, fishing, snowmobiling, and skiing. No one schedules work for the first week of deer hunting. It's an area that has traditionally been populated by men who work shifts in manufacturing or papermaking. I've noticed something peculiar over the years—that friendships of the classical sort are more frequent where formal education is lower. It seems that the more education we have, the more introspective and analytical we tend to be about our relationships, and the more we analyze and measure our relationships.

At one point several years ago, my family was facing severe financial difficulty due to changes in the economy. That was compounded by legal issues with the way our home had been built a decade before we bought it, and with the soundness of the bank that held our mortgage. We were facing the possible loss of our home. I shared this with a few close friends, and the result was striking.

---

* See Sherwin Nuland: *How We Die*. Nuland was a pathologist who wrote a book detailing the physical process of death. He believed that by pathologizing death, making death a failure of the medical system, and removing death from life itself, we have lost much of our appreciation for life. Nuland attributed the proliferation of crimes against others, particularly murder, to the loss of the value of life itself, peculiar to Western literate cultures.

My church friends told me I should go to their food bank and assistance ministry, where we could get expired and surplus food along with counseling. Another friend, who had never set foot in my church, offered us the use of their lake home for as long as we needed it if we lost our home. One offered food that had been donated to them by companies seeking a tax write-off, while the other offered shelter with no questions asked. One offered a way to fix *me*, while the other offered shelter.

Like the disciples when they encountered the man born blind, the first question from my church friends was who was at fault. The disciples asked, "Who sinned? Him or his parents?" My church friends, meaning well, offered counseling to help me figure out why I was encountering difficulty. My non-church friend immediately looked to what they could do to help us through a difficult time. They seemed to accept that tough times just happen, through no fault of our own, and that the best response was to share what they had to help us.

Tension Between Two Worlds: Friendship

1. Describe your relationship with your best friend from childhood. Was it more like modern friendship or ancient?

2. Do you have any enduring friendships that don't depend on trading self-disclosure leading to self-affirmation? What are they like?

3. Can you accept the offer of friendship with Jesus?

4. How would our marriages be different if we were friends with our spouses?

5. How would our walk with Christ change if we were to understand the invitation of friendship?

6. Would a community based on friendship be more satisfying than one based on exchange of personal information?

7. Would replacing modern for ancient friendship change how we feel about guilt in our ongoing walk?

7
Models, Metaphors, and Mysteries

We all know that the brain controls the body by connecting to the extremities through the central nervous system. Much like a telephone, the senses send messages to the brain, and the brain sends messages back to the muscles through the nervous system. The brain acts like a central control or switchboard, sending messages that move our hands away from the danger of a hot stove and toward the danger of a chocolate bunny.

Like Mission Control at NASA, the brain controls the body through sending and receiving messages. We've seen this model in our eighth-grade science book, parodied countless times in comedy movies and shows, and if we're old enough, we might remember the old science films sponsored by Bell Labs with the bald guy explaining it all. Again, if we're old enough, we might remember this description from the old *Reader's Digest* "I am Joe's..." body part series of articles in the 1960s and 1970s.

It would make sense for us to understand communication the same way. It's what we've been taught, and what's been reinforced by our continued use of the terms belonging to the model, over and over, until it becomes reality. The brain devises a message, sends it to the extremities, and waits for a response confirming receipt of the message without distortion.

We've even used it to describe the meaning of Paul's metaphor of the Body of Christ. Each of us is a part of the body, contributing what's needed for the benefit of the body. Jesus is the head (brain) sending messages through the nervous system (ministry). Each of us needs to be in touch with the brain through prayer, reporting back what we're seeing and experiencing so that the brain can send direction through the ministry. Our churchy metaphors still echo an understanding of the church as a unique form of technology and our involvement as part of the design. We're invited to "connect," or to "plug in," to what a church is doing. We learn that we are all "wired differently," or that some things are "hardwired into our brains." We need time to "process" the information we've just heard, and if we're having a bad day, we are encouraged to "set our thermostat to praise, instead of the default setting of worry." And who can forget this classic worship song, which can still be found in hymnals in many of our local churches. As you read the words, think of "supercalifragilisticexpialidocious" from Mary Poppins:

Chorus
Telephone to glory, oh, what joy divine!
I can feel the current moving on the line
Made by God the Father for His very own,
You may talk to Jesus on this royal telephone.

Central's never busy, always on the line,
You can hear from heaven almost any time.
'Tis a royal service, built for one and all,
When you get in trouble, give this royal line a call. (chorus)

There will be no charges, telephone is free.
It is built for service, just for you and me.

There will be no waiting on this royal line,
Telephone to glory always answers just in time. (chorus)

Fail to get the answer, Satan's crossed your wire
By some strong delusion, or some base desire;
Take away obstructions, God is on the throne,
And you'll get your answer through this royal telephone. (chorus)

If your line is "grounded," and connection true
Has been lost with Jesus, tell you what to do:
Prayer and faith and promise mend the broken wire,
Till your soul is burning with the Pentecostal fire. (Chorus)

Carnal combinations cannot get control
Of this line to glory, anchored in the soul;
Storm and trial cannot disconnect the line,
Held in constant keeping by the Father's hand divine.

This was written in 1919, and while it seems quaint today, it was recorded and released as recently as 2009. Before cell phone technology, phones were physically wired and subject to a host of interruptions and distortions that were so common that users devised their own vocabulary to describe them.

Not only do we know how the brain works, but we understand how it stores memories. We know, for instance, that the brain stores memories in localized areas, and that certain areas of the brain control separate functions of the body. The prefrontal cortex, for instance, is the seat of reasoning and restraint. Damage this through chronic traumatic encephalopathy, and irrational and unpredictable behavior follows. Damage to the brain by stroke or other forms of traumatic injury can remove those abilities.

There's only one problem with this understanding of how the brain interfaces with the body. It's not correct! The technology of brain machine interface is one application of the science of neurophysiology. The goal of this dedicated group of scientists is to develop neuroprosthetics, which are artificial limbs that can be controlled by the brain. In order to design and develop artificial limbs that move and behave in a lifelike manner, scientists must first understand how the brain controls the human limb. And it's here that challenges arise.

In one stunning development, researchers found that the muscle fibers begin contracting *before* a signal is sent from the brain. It's as if the muscles themselves begin contracting in anticipation of receiving a message to do so. This completely blows our understanding of the brain as the origin of the signal out of the water! In another challenge, researchers are still unsure whether the memories are stored in local areas or distributed across the entire brain. The processing of impulses seems to be distributed across the brain, so that in some instances it takes place everywhere and nowhere in the brain.

Scientists are still developing models to even begin to describe the complexity they are finding in as simple a task as a rat moving a single whisker in response to a morsel of food. Understanding this simple task alone requires the use of supercomputers that don't even exist yet. What if we were to apply these new findings to our understanding of the Body of Christ? That the connection of the cell to the brain may be such that muscles prepare to move in anticipation of an impulse through the nervous system, and that the nervous system confirms the movement and reinforces it?

This is how models work in science: researchers devise them to help us understand complex processes in simple terms. In doing so, they must decide what is part of the process and what isn't part of the process. They make assumptions about what to include in the model and what to exclude as part of the process. Then, further research is conducted based on an understanding of the process as reflected in the simplified model. Findings confirm or disconfirm the model, and the terms of the model become part of the vocabulary of the researchers.

When the models become part of our introductory textbooks, they are simplified even further, and when they are adopted without question by those who popularize the academic models for public consumption, they become even more reduced and simplified. When we begin to write songs using the models, we reduce them even more. We end up with theology as an earwig. Along the way, the models change from tentative, such as, "This is our best understanding at the moment…maybe," to "Not only is this the truth, its God's truth. Truth with a capital T. And it's what Paul had in mind two thousand years ago. This is how the Creator of all things relates to us."

A keen listener might realize that models of communication are really descriptions of dominant technologies. Shannon's model using the fairly new technology of the telephone didn't pay much attention to the non-verbal elements of conversation. The model treats what we see, feel, smell, and hear while we're chatting as distractions. It doesn't take into account our energy level after a good night's sleep, our attitude after the last conversation didn't go so well, or our tone. These are all relegated to the status of "noise." And no wonder. The model didn't change much until television became common.

The watershed year for television was 1954, which was the year that TV ownership reached 50 percent of US households. The need to account for the visual and non-verbal elements was driven by the proliferation of a new technology. In fact, the study of non-verbal communication doesn't come up until after Shannon's basic model was expanded to account for the amazing new experience that TV could bring. When Fredrick Lehman wrote "The Royal Telephone" in 1919, this was cutting-edge technology. Alexander Graham Bell had patented his design for a telephone in 1876, and universal phone systems were not available. The Communications Act of 1934 was the first federal recognition of the value of a national telephone system. That act had, as its goal, "making available, so far as possible, to all the people of the United States… a rapid, efficient, nationwide and worldwide wire and radio communication service with adequate facilities at reasonable charges..."*

It wasn't until 1948 that a bill was passed that provided low-interest loans for rural telephone systems, as an extension of the Rural Electrification Act. This put a different light on Claude Shannon's effort to eliminate distortion and signal degradation when he published his mathematical model of communication in 1949. This was cutting-edge thinking, as trendy and forward thinking as the development of theologies of widely dispersed and interconnected communities today, based on cloud computing.

It's not uncommon to hear our relationship to the Father explained using computer terms, as computers have become common in our homes and in our pockets. Just this morning, I read a daily devotion that comes to my inbox, discussing how we can hear God's voice in our everyday work life (an "inbox" in my pocket—what's that?). This particular writer focuses on putting faith into practice at work, and is read by many who follow what has become known as the "Faith at Work" movement.

> One of the great mysteries of the universe to my logical mind is how God can communicate with six billion people on the earth at the same time. It is one of those mysteries I must let go of because my "hard drive" would crash if I had to explain and understand this before I believed and trusted in Him. It is as though God places a computer chip in each human being, and when we place our faith and trust in Him it becomes activated. We begin to communicate with Him...Sin can create a poor frequency in our communication with the Shepherd. Make sure your frequency is free of static

---

* Communications Act of 1934, *https://transition.fcc.gov/Reports/1934new.pdf*, 1.

(sin) today so that the Shepherd can lead you and go before you.*

The writer uses metaphors of both radio and computer to explain the relationship that sheep have with their shepherd. Human thought is modeled like computer function, and the self is modeled as hardware. The mind functions like a computer, with the potential to be overloaded by too many calculations at once. The reader is encouraged to see their connection to God through the metaphor of two different types of technology. And in fact, this description has itself become outdated.

If written today, ten years later, we'd craft a sermon describing the frustration of seeing a cell tower in a verdant green field next to the highway as we drive, but having our signal drop as we're handed from tower to tower. We can see it, we know the connection should be strongest the closer we are to the tower, and yet we simply can't be heard. We might get clever and proclaim that everyone wants 5G, but we really need one big G only. We might even cry out in anguish, "My carrier, my carrier, why has thou dropped me?" (If written before electronically mediated communication technologies were invented, would we have said, "My pigeon, my pigeon, why didst thou plummet from the skies"?)

At any moment in history, we can look at sermon texts and figure out where it stands in the progression of technology. We can hear the terms of the newest technology used to explain theological concepts. We can infer the terms of the old technology by what the speaker proposes to change. And we can even predict where society is headed as new technologies emerge.

---

*   Hillman, Os. "Hearing His Voice." *Today God is First.* March 22, 2022. https://todaygodisfirst.com/hearing-his-voice/

Literacy and Single Meanings

All stories have lessons in them. Most of the good ones have many lessons, like the parables told by Jesus, and the lessons are helpful depending on where we are when we hear the story. One of the biggest losses happens when custom and tradition reduce multiple meanings to one meaning only. The meanings are often based on our own assumptions about how the world works.

When the singular meaning is used as the foundation of a theology, we concretize the meaning of the story further. And the meanings that we take from them are shaped by the thought processes that have arisen through primary literacy. Seldom do we think about how the *sound* of the voice might give us broader understanding. Sometimes, the sound of the words spoken can even challenge our traditions about what might have been heard.

For instance, I recently heard a sermon on the story of Peter walking on the water. The preacher developed the thought that we need to be like Peter, willing to stand out, and willing to take a risk, because his faith wasn't like the faith of the others who stayed in the boat. The speaker was careful to make the point that Peter's faith wasn't superior to the other disciples', just different. Of course, the difference was one to be desired, to the point that the speaker said that he wanted God to give him a holy discontent for the status quo. We all know that showing us a difference is because the difference matters. Who can imagine a sermon where we hear a difference that doesn't matter? Chief among the lessons to be learned was that we must embrace our uniqueness, and while we shouldn't seek to be better, we should aspire to be different.

The sermon reinforced many of the tenets of modern individualism in a literate culture, as we've discussed earlier. It's about the lesson I derive, which is about me and how I compare to the others in the boat. Like we've asked about other examples, how would this sound to an oral ear? Would we find the same lesson—that it isn't enough to be in the boat? That being with the eleven is somehow a failure? That our lack of faith by staying in the boat is a disappointment to our Maker? That our individualism is paramount? Rather than accepting our lives as the tapestry of God's handiwork, we regard everything about ourselves as displeasing?

Or would the oral thinker hear something different in the whole story? That the disciples were in the boat against their will, having been *ordered* by Jesus to get in the boat and start crossing the sea? Would the oral ear, connected to nature, note that these were men who spent their lives on the water, and were perfectly aware of the kind of conditions where a storm would come up? That not wanting to get in the boat was a matter of wisdom, and getting into the boat was a matter of faith and obedience?

Would the oral ear listener recall that every time Jesus got near a boat, strange and unsettling things happened? Would an oral ear have noted that their fears were confirmed by the storm that arose? Would an oral ear have heard that Peter's response when they all recognized Jesus was to try to change the story from being about Jesus to being about Peter? ("If it's really you, let *me* do it.") Would an oral ear hear that Jesus didn't call Peter to do anything, that Peter challenged Jesus to prove His identity to Peter's satisfaction, and that Jesus' response was just one word?

How many ways can a parent say, "Okay. Go ahead," to an unruly and unpredictable toddler who has just said, "Let me do it"? And who was Jesus looking at when He said what He did? Would an oral ear have heard Jesus words "why did you doubt" as being directed to Peter, who separated himself from the crowd, or to the disciples who stayed in the boat? Would an oral thinker hear that Jesus was commending those who risked their lives by being in the boat through faith and obedience, while Peter was the one who made it about himself?

In short, an oral thinker could hear the story as a reinforcement of the truth that the nail that stands out is the one that gets pounded down. Peter's insistence on standing out was what led him to the failure, while those who stayed in the boat were saved and saw a demonstration of Jesus's mastery over the natural world. An oral thinker might even hear in this an echo of Psalm 107:23–30:

> Some went out on the sea in ships; they were merchants on the mighty waters. They saw the works of the LORD, his wonderful deeds in the deep. For he spoke and stirred up a tempest that lifted high the waves. They mounted up to the heavens and went down to the depths; in their peril their courage melted away. They reeled and staggered like drunkards; they were at their wits end. Then they cried out to the LORD in their trouble, and he brought them out of their distress. He stilled the storm to a whisper; the waves of the sea were hushed. They were glad when it grew calm, and he guided them to their desired haven. (NIV)

In short, an oral thinker could hear in this story the reinforcement of the very thing that modern preachers denigrate: a collective sense of self. I struggle as I write this, because the first words I used were "a reinforcement of group conformity." I changed the phrase, as the term *conformity* has such negative connotations to the modern ear.

The story of Peter is one of those Bible stories that can be used to reinforce all sorts of poor ideas. "Let's build a bigger building. Why? Because Jesus doesn't want us to just stay in the boat. He wants us to step out in faith." Yes, but why do we need a bigger building instead of encouraging twenty or thirty of our members to start supporting another smaller, struggling church in our town? "Because staying in the boat is a failure." Maybe it's cynicism, but every time I hear the text announced, I wonder what ask is coming. Peter may be the first person to be put into a dunk tank; every time we need money, Peter has to get wet.

The story of Peter is our go-to for motivating people to act, whether it's the best thing to do or not. Even if we don't cite Peter, the metaphors of our faith experience still echo the story. We "step out in faith." We "step out of the boat." And each time we call ourselves to faith like Peter, we tell ourselves that the faith of a mustard seed isn't enough. Isn't it strange that if we ask people what the story is about, the title most of us know it by is "this is where Peter walks on the water"? Not "this is where Jesus demonstrates that even the seas obey His command"?

Even the editors of our Bible identify the story that way in their chapter subheadings. Yet of the three accounts to be found in the New Testament, only one mentions Peter, while two simply have Jesus calming the waters. All three note that the disciples were on the scene against their will, having been ordered to set out in a small boat on the cusp of a storm. So of the eleven who observed, only one noticed, or only one thought that Peter's actions were worth sharing. It's ironic that what the disciples didn't think worth mentioning is what we tell ourselves we must aspire to emulate.

Speculations on Modern Friendship

I raised the question in the last chapter about how different our teaching might be if it were based on an oral understanding of Scripture rather than a literate one. Would it sound and look the same? What would teaching about marriage sound like if we were to use an oral, classical understanding of friendship as the ultimate relationship that Jesus offers to us, instead of the modern-day poker game played over the telephone? What would it look like if we used classical friendship as the glue that holds our church community together? Space doesn't permit a full treatment, but we can speculate. It might look something like this:

1. Jesus exemplified a number of relationships. The highest of these was *friend*. To invite someone into friendship is to offer a commitment of three major elements: promising that "I will take

pleasure in your company, offering all I have for your use and committing everything to helping you work out practical wisdom and balance in your life. It's a commitment to *your* blessing, not to having my needs met."

2. That commitment transcends just the exchange of secrets and unknown information. It's the ultimate expression of mutual respect and consideration, born of the desire for equality. Friendship can forgive without excusing, and encourage you to grow up. Friendship persists in the face of disappointment, continues long after discomfort, and even persists after betrayal. Friendship is a commitment that can span generations, and my children can be bound by the pact. Friendship goes way beyond feeling and judgment. Friendship doesn't end, because it doesn't have the conditions of terminating within it. Classical friendship won't leave and won't forsake, while modern friendship always looks for a way out. Modern friendship, and in fact all modern relationships, have the conditions of leaving and unbridgeable distance baked into them.

3. Instead of viewing communication as a tool to get you to think like me, or as an expression of my inner person, or to exercise power in an asymmetrical fashion, we'd find some other way to think about what happens when we use words. We might model communication as a dance. We could (as some ancients did) model communication as a form of playful sword battle, or even as wrestling. Many of the metaphors that we use in conversation echo these alternatives. We say, "What's your point? What's the thrust of the argument? She parried by saying this. It was a brilliant riposte." All terms still used in fencing. We could look at communication as the ability to find the right *kinds* of things to say that smooth over the bumps and needs of a given situation, with the attention given to helping the other people in the conversation. All of these keep an outward rather than an

inward focus, and all of them put the other person's understanding or good as the desired outcome of the conversation. They don't differentiate between the "real" person and the outward acts. They don't separate our words from our character. We are humans, not machines exchanging electrons.

4. Our relationship is built on shared understanding, not each of us having our needs met first. "I care about your needs, and you care about mine. I put everything at your disposal. I prefer to be with you; I look for ways to make our time together enjoyable. In any conversation, you are more important than I am. It's not about being understood; it's about understanding. We don't even need to understand each other; I seek to understand you." This can be as simple as deciding that in every conversation, my purpose is to build you up. Like Paul, I won't open my mouth unless it's to edify. And like the psalmist, I'll ask the Lord to set a watch on my heart so that my words might be pleasing to Him, who is the third party in our friendship.

5. "We make the same commitment to each other, but I will focus on your part in the friendship. If you betray, like Judas, I'll still offer forgiveness. If you run, like Peter, I'll still be there. If you curse me, like Peter, I'll still offer you bread and fish on the shore, and I'll say what you need to hear to restore your joy. If you tell me to leave, like Naomi, I'll say, 'Let your home be my home, and your people my people. You're stuck with me.'" The commitment of friendship doesn't have a freshness date on the bottom of the label.

6. We may encounter difficulty along the way, but we understand that together, we are woven into a friendship with Jesus. That means that our commitment to working out His purposes might involve challenges and troubles along the way. Those are an unavoidable part of helping Him carry out His best intentions for His creation. So the troubles won't be about us; they'll be

about us fulfilling our promises of friendship with Him. If sickness comes, it may be so that He can minister to someone in the doctor's waiting room, and sickness puts us next to them. If death comes to one of us, as it always will, we'll rejoice in the time He gave us, and our grief at the loss will be tempered by knowing that our friend is home and safe, and that we've fulfilled our promise.

7. If God gives us children, our goal will be to raise them to become friends of God. Yes, for now they need help with skinned knees and basic reasoning, but ultimately, we want them to grow to become women and men of character. Through a long process of maturing, we will make the offer of eventual complete friendship. What will be lacking in the early days is the element of mutuality in the relationship. Our hope is that in time, like the prodigal, they may be able to accept the offer, go beyond the first two promises, and stand face-to-face with us, no matter how much they've messed up along the way. When our children were babies, my nightly practice before putting them in the crib was to pray that God would become their friend, in the fullness of all that means, all the days of their lives. I would pray (and still do) that friendship with Him would span their generations, to their children and their children's children. I believe that prayer will go way beyond just praying for their well-being, and I'm excited and eager to see how God will work it out in their adulthood.

8. "This kind of relationship isn't about power. It's not about balancing power. It's about laying power down. It's about giving power away. You are more important than me. In every conversation, it's more important to care about your well-being than my own. In every conversation, my goal is to build you up. If I can't truly say that, I won't enter into a formal legal relationship with you." Again, it's the mutuality of the commitment that makes it go beyond just giving and receiving.

As we can see from just this brief description, a marriage seminar built around these concepts would be far different than discussing the Johari Window. I'm not here to discover who I really am based on what I think the other person might see about me that I miss. A pre-marriage counseling workshop would go way beyond discussing what *my* expectations are going into marriage, and how they might conflict with yours. And it might be different in that it would emphasize that a promise of friendship, once given, isn't rescinded because I'm not getting more out of the relationship than I'm putting into it.

Friendship and Community

These days, we make much of admitting our failures and weaknesses. I can't turn on the local station without hearing songs that proclaim that it's okay not to be okay, as if we enter into God's presence by self-denigration rather than by the blood of Jesus. What seems to unite us is the fact that we're all "broken" and needy, and willing and eager to say so. We've come to think that to do less is to be dishonest. Perhaps one of the reasons we overlook true friendship is because of the way we hear Jesus' words. He says that He has told us everything, and we are His friends if we do what He asks. The conditional and confessional nature of the verses are what we hear, filtered through the tradition of monastic life. In the history of friendship, the greatest contribution seems to be that of transparency, not because transparency is required between us and God, but because monastic life demands all of the details.

Casual, non-vocational church membership doesn't have the same requirements. But the emphasis on telling everything as a mark of our Christian dedication arises centuries after Jesus' day. We tell ourselves that they'll know us by our transparency, while the New Testament writers tell us that they'll know us by our love for one another, and by our moderation (practical experiential wisdom).

In a similar way, we hear Jesus' words through the filter of having all things in common, and in the forced sharing of material resources made necessary by persecution. This sharing is a reaction to outside political forces, whereas common encouragement already exists by virtue of being called out. An ancient oral world wouldn't have heard the conditional nature of the statement like we would. We hear it as "I'll be your friend if you tell me everything and if you do what I ask," meaning that if we stop self-disclosing, He'll stop being our friend. And we hear "You are my friends if you do what I ask" to reinforce *actions* as the key to gaining His friendship. This is a modern conception of friendship, based on self-disclosure and works. What kind of friendship is this that we can turn it on or off?

One of the "god terms" of the current culture is *community*." By "god term," I mean a term that has such positive associations that it can't be questioned. We have such positive feelings about the word that we don't question anything offered to us if the word *community* is used as part of the appeal. And who can argue with something that's good for the community? Like hating Grandma, disagreeing with you if you have the community in mind is a rhetorical landmine. Just for fun, listen to how many times the word is used in any news story, or how often it's repeated during the evening news. It's not uncommon to hear the word used multiple ways in the same story, none of them specific.

But what is a community? How does it form, and what constitutes a community? I joke with my students that if you have a hobby, it's a statistic. If you share the hobby with a friend, it's a coincidence. If three of you like to do it, it's become a community. So if you like to wear flannel boxers while watching *Star Trek* reruns, that's just you. If two people do it, you may have a coincidence. If three or more of you do it, you have a community. If you're politically minded, you might form a group and assert your rights as the FBWSTRWC (Flannel Boxer Wearing *Star Trek* Rerun Watching Community).

The process of gaining power is to define yourself as a community by telling us that you're different. And in post-postmodern thought, any difference is an indication of a power differential, and any difference in power is bad, and the result of oppressive mechanisms in your culture. Thus, watching *Star Trek* reruns in your flannel boxers becomes a political act, which pushes back against the oppressive hegemonic forces of flannelphobia.

In modern terms, a community is an imaginary group of people that I construct through my appeals when I want to persuade you of something, or when I want to prevent you from opposing me. If it's "for the community," it can't be opposed, much like we were told as kids that we should never hit someone who is wearing glasses. Put them on, and you can say whatever you like. *Community* is a warm fuzzy term used to gain assent without asking for it, and to prevent even the discussion of merit. From that stance, we can demand access to power. I can argue that we look down on people who wear flannel boxers, and that we need more of us in engineering. Presumably, people who wear flannel boxers do the math to build bridges differently than people who don't do the boxer thing.

While this may be the path to power, it doesn't answer the question of what a community is in today's terms. Community can mean the city, town, or political unit you live in, such as "the greater Green Bay community." It could mean all of the people who share your interests, passions, or commitments. The motorcycle community. The collector car community. The Beanie Baby collectors' community. It could mean the political positions you hold in common with other people. It could mean the advocacy group you belong to, or the magazine readership you're part of, or the hobby for which you spend free time. Or it could simply be what you call yourself in order to escape negative associations with a given denomination: "We're _____ Community Church, not First ___ Church."

We have a bank in our region that uses the term in multiple ways in the same ad. "Community Bank, in the community because we care about the community." I cringe every time I hear it, because it uses so many empty phrases and does it in such a short time. "In a Thomas Kinkade version of community, kindness is more than just a word on a pillow. We have relationships with the butcher on the corner. Real people. Real conversations. Nicolet Bank." Ignoring the obvious fact that there are only eight butcher shops within a fifty-mile radius of the station, and most of those aren't on corners in residential neighborhoods, the bank makes its appeals by contrasting itself with all of the other banks out there. Those other banks are full of empty conversations and fake people who have no relationships.

By now, we should be asking, "What do you mean by relationship? Fake? Real?" When the teller at the drive-up asks me if I want any particular size bills when I cash a check, do they really mean it? "How about them Cubbies? That'll be fifty cents extra for human service."

Self, Community, and Orality

What if we were to understand and teach about our identity in oral terms? That we are who we are not because we're separate, distant, always trying to bridge the gap, and always failing because we can't reconcile our inner and outer selves? What if we saw ourselves as being brought to life by being redeemed—now part of the Body of Believers, and taking our identity from Him? Would that help fill the loneliness that is baked into our contemporary understandings? Would it allow us to sit at His feet, knowing that He'll never leave us, rather than us always seeking His presence that always seems to be slipping away? Would it allow us to live lives of quiet confidence, where we wouldn't feel as if our brokenness is all He sees?

Would it allow us to accept our past for what it is: the treasured steps planned and ordered by a loving Father to bring us to His grace?

To go back to the song about honesty, we're told in our popular theology that we're broken, and that disclosure is the only way to fix our brokenness. Contrast this with Paul's terms when he addresses who and what we are. We're not "broken" before coming to know Christ. We're dead. We aren't fixed, we're raised to newness of life. If we're part of the Body of Christ, having been redeemed by His blood, we're not "broken." We're complete in Him who is the head of all principalities and powers.

We love the metaphor of brokenness, because it puts the solution back in our hands. We fix things that are broken, while we bury things that are dead. Fixing means that I have a solution, that I can envision a set of steps, or a workshop, a brochure, or even a book that describes how things can be repaired. But being dead is different. I have no solution to death. Like Martha and Mary, I can only grieve in the face of death, and cry to God, "You could have healed him!" And like Martha and Mary, I could marvel and rejoice when Lazarus is brought back to life. I can't explain it. The modern view of language, self, and God thus turns us from seekers into tweakers.

Here's how we might teach about community from an oral perspective:

1. I'm a member of the Body of Christ, having been born again and redeemed by His blood. I've been adopted into His family, and it's this family that gives me my identity. I'm no longer struggling to define who I am against a hostile world; I am who I am because I'm made in His image. My place and my role are defined by the needs of others and the gifts that God has placed in my heart, and the fact that I'm in this subgroup tells me that there is a need for what I can contribute. Instead of a collection of uneasy, flawed individuals making up a community of flawed discontent, we are joined together by God such that nothing is lacking.

2. God has given the potential for close friendships in this group. I like being together with you, I'm willing to share what God has given me, and I'm willing to commit what I have to helping this

group work out balance, moderation, and practical wisdom in everything that it does. I don't go to church to get something; I go to share with others what I've received from Him during the week as He shows His goodness and mercy.

3. I can't make this commitment to other groups, or even to a large group for that matter, but I can make it to a small group of people who I associate with more closely. Like a small group, a cell group, a prayer group, or a men's group.

4. My involvement in those small groups is through the commitments of what I bring, not because I'm searching for a self that exists separately from the group. It's not even for what I can get from the group; it's what I can bring. My commitment isn't measured by transparency, by honesty, or by the quantity of information I share about myself. I'm not of interest here; you are, and the group takes precedence over self. I benefit because the group does. There's a well known allegory which describes hell as being like sitting at a banquet table, with forks attached to your hands that were longer than the distance from your plate to your mouth. You couldn't eat because the fork and knife were too long, so the banqueter's starved in the presence of abundance. Heaven, on the other hand, was the same banquet where the people realized that the only way they could eat was to feed each other.*

5. My loyalty will probably be to the small group over the larger collection of groups that make up the bigger church, just like my connection to the local church will be stronger than my connection to the Body of Christ on a regional or national level. Yet the

---

* This allegory exists in many traditions including Jewish, Hindu, Buddhist, Middle Eastern, and Christian. It's a perfect example of how the technology of literacy shifts our questions from experience to ownership. A Google search for "Parable of the spoons" lists over 11 million hits, and the search for "origin" of the parable lists over 430,000 articles trying to determine where the parable was first written down, constituting the "real" version.

potential still exists that I can find friendships among the larger group as well. My eyes will always be open, and my ears will always listen, for the opportunity to build you up.

6. I'll hear and understand Scriptures through the filter of oral community, not the individual self first. The Scriptures were spoken to oral communities, not to individuals in isolation. They were communal stories meant to be heard in groups. This might broaden our understanding of some of the more difficult passages, which weren't dictated to the heroic individual in the first place. For instance, on the issue of predestination, we always ask, "How can God, who knows everything, know what my future choices will be and still grant me free will?" Because Paul wrote that we are predestined to salvation. Yet if we understand this through the collective community first, it's not a problem. God has predestined the *Body* for His purposes, and I'm part of the body. The bus is going to the destination, and my choice is to get on the bus. The bus isn't going to the destination because I get on it. *Hearing* Scripture through the filter of orality, spoken and declared to the community, rather than just reading it in isolation and asking what it means to me, enriches our understanding. It's as simple as asking what God is saying to *us*, and by extension to me, rather than what He's saying to *me*, and maybe to us as a collection of individuals who share common goals or hobbies.

7. It would change how we look at hardship. Instead of asking why this is happening to us and trying to fix it, we might ask what I can do to help you. We've talked at length about faithfulness instead of success, and how it's not about me...*ever*. It's about His purposes in our life, and the lives of those He has brought us next to.

8. Finally, how would friendship with Him change the way we look at prayer and intercession? We're taught to pray, and

there's a selflessness in what Jesus taught us. What if we understood prayer not as us logging time with Him, bringing Him our concerns, or letting Him in on things that are happening that He might not be aware of? What if we saw it as more than continual knocking on the door of a friend who is ignoring us, or embarrassing a crooked judge into doing what is right? Instead of seeing ourselves as part of the nervous system, reporting back to the head, what if we understood ourselves as sitting in the door of our tent, in the heat of the day, when the Lord seeks us out for comfort, fellowship, sustenance, and maybe even to stand in His face to plead for mercy to prevail over justice? What if we saw the times that we wake out of sleep with someone on our heart, as our Friend letting us in on His discomfort, allowing us to feel His grief, and inviting us to offer Him comfort? What if we understood prayer to be like with Adam and Eve, where the Lord sought *them* out to walk with His voice in the cool of the day?

It may seem, at the end of the story, that I am attacking modern psychology and the influence it has had in furnishing the models for human motivation, communication, and community. I'm not. Our teaching has benefited greatly from some of the insights brought by modernity. But there's also an echo, underneath it all, that perhaps what we hear every morning as we listen to our favorite Christian station, when we tune in to our favorite online preacher, or even when we hear the teaching of our busy local pastors, that what we hear may not be quite the same as what those who heard Paul's letters read aloud might have heard.

We live our modern lives by theories put forth by experts. Oral cultures depended on tradition and the weight of accumulated wisdom to decide what was good, while we live by reference to what the experts say is true. It's inescapable, and one of the ironies is that I've relied on experts throughout this story to buttress my opinion, when I thought you needed to hear my point from someone older and wiser than I. We rely on the theories, and all of our theories work the same way.

They begin with the assumption that something is wrong, and collect data to support the assumption by working toward healing those who are afflicted. When people improve, we associate what we've done with people getting better. We then use the contours of what was wrong to define what is right and functional. Like Freud, we begin with a pathology, infer a cause, and work to remove the cause. If it seems to work, we define "normal" as the absence of the pathology. We then generalize that theory of normal behavior or normal being to all people everywhere, rather than realizing that we may be imposing our own experience upon all of humanity across time.

For example, dyslexia is a condition that is now recognized, but prior to the advent of literacy, it didn't exist. In its simplest terms, it lies in the brain's ability to order and sequence marks on the page. Prior to the development of compulsory education and the advent of primary literacy, only specialists relied on black marks on a flat paper surface to convey critical information. But once literacy became the norm, and we thought that everything worth knowing resides in written form, we feel compelled to call the inability to gain meaning from the page a disorder, and a threat to living a productive life. The lack of tools to adapt to a new form of technology thus becomes pathologized as a disorder of the brain, requiring treatment.

This would be like convincing the church that all sermons must be sung, and then marking those who lack the requisite musical ability as unfit for the pulpit. Even today, as we struggle to understand the thought processes and values of a generation raised on the internet, we're starting to define "good" ministerial candidates based on their ability to navigate the narcissosphere.

The Tension Between Two Worlds

Modern-day Christians are a discontent people, largely because we've taught ourselves to be discontent. We've gotten there through two retro readings, which arise through the filter of literacy overlaid on an oral experience. We teach ourselves to disparage our past, and to yearn for a perfect future that we can only imagine but never attain. Then, we teach ourselves to turn away from deep friendship with the Father and each other, in order to pursue thin friendships based on the exchange of information, and base all relationships on a thin model of romance.

We see our past behind us, rejected by God and the source of our shame, and we yearn for our vision of something better. We call it faith, thinking that we're doing what Paul tells us we should do, but it's really rejecting what God has done for and in us, while yearning for what He hasn't done and probably won't do. At the same time, we reject true friendship with the Father and a small circle of others, in favor of the exchange model of machine-like intimacy. We are cut off from the very things that would bring us joy, celebrating who we are and where we've come from, while being centered in a circle of trusted friends who would lay down all they have to help us become what God desires for us.

Our modern culture, our political systems, and our entertainment all teach us to live this way. Every two or four years, we reject our past as flawed and vote for what is new. Every New Year's Day, we ring out the old, putting it behind us, and ring in the new. Each generation blames the one that came before it for the evils that we discover in our world. The new is celebrated over the old, much like the current love of science, engineering, technology, and math, which misses the irony that the current mess that the earth finds itself in is because of the accumulated byproducts of processes invented by previous generations of scientists, engineers, technology creators, and mathematicians.

Often, the relationships to which we aspire are the opposite of what first-century believers would have prized. In a set of testimonies about a men's Bible study that I heard recently, the most important elements of connection were transparency, honesty, accountability, and lack of judgment. Each of the men talked about how opening up and sharing their secrets led to them feeling like they weren't alone. Each talked about how the element of risk was involved—the fear that their experiences would be rejected and judged, and that they'd be left alone in their pain. They all reflected a modern sense of friendship—that friendship arises from the sharing of personal information at the risk of rejection. To withhold personal information is to remain dishonest, unhealthy, and alone, and to share is to begin the process of healing. If we don't share our deepest pain, we are deceiving ourselves and others, and if we don't tell everything, we're lying.

Notice how this echoes a modern sense of how the Lord works in our lives, and how thin our relationship is to God? We may be released from our sin by the sacrifice of our Savior, but we still carry our pain. We may be exonerated, but we're still broken, helpless, and alone. We may be forgiven, but we're still incomplete until we tell each other our secrets. We may be released from bondage to sin, but we're still in bondage to the consequences of the sins of others. We're not healed, but we're introduced to an environment where somehow, if we risk enough, others can help us heal ourselves.

The price of admission to the game is the disclosure of our emotional state. At the end, we may find a place where we're no longer judged, but until then we must continue to disclose ourselves in an endless game of risk. And each time we get together, we have to find some new tidbit to share. Each time we get together could be our last, the moment when we finally share something too personal or too repugnant, and then we're back to being alone and judged.

Contrast this with friendship in oral cultures and moments. We are part of the Body of Christ because He has adopted us. He washes us, cleanses us, and makes us whole. Together, we are complete in Him who is the head of all principalities and powers. We commit ourselves to one another, in reciprocal pledges of mutual care and support, to make increase of the Body in love. Judgment is involved, but not judgment of one another and the path by which God has led us to His people. We celebrate your path, even if we don't know the details. Instead, our judgment is a commitment that we will help you do whatever you need to help you grow into what God has spoken for you.

We judge sin to be dead because Jesus took sin to the cross. We're happy to help you identify and put away the patterns of your old life—the trained incapacities that you learned in order to survive. The no-judgment zone we seek isn't because we've built it by sharing our pain; it exists because we commit to one another *first* that no experience is too extreme for our sense of what God can do. In other words, we don't arrive at acceptance because we've played the right card; we are accepted as friends first because Jesus has been our friend. We commit to friendship *first* because He is our friend, and we will never leave you nor forsake you. Risk of rejection is gone, because He will never reject us, just as He never rejected Peter, Judas, and the others who betrayed or rejected Him.

Niobe Way shows us something interesting in her book about friendships among inner-city youth. People instinctively form the kinds of friendships that sustain and nurture us, up until the time we are taught something else. When I've discussed the evolution of friendship in classes or workshops, I've seen that this isn't just common among Way's subjects. Audiences, when asked to describe their own experiences of friendship, have described something much more like the classic relationship than the exchange model of Knapp and other modern thinkers. Everyone seems to have had a childhood friend who was closer than a sibling, with whom one shared everything and to whom one offered the same access. But as we grow older and we learn more about how we're supposed to navigate the complexities of human relationships, those friends disappear. We kill them off. We may even quote Paul about putting away childhood friendships to ourselves when we do this, and tell ourselves that we've put away childish things.

But here lies a paradox. The more we know about modern friendships, and the more we analyze and dissect their origins and dynamics, the less satisfying our friendships become. As Way shows us, the loss of those early friendships is strongly associated with enormous costs in terms of mental and physical well-being. And as the advent of Facebook friends seems to demonstrate, the more friends we have, the more isolated we feel.

Could it be, that like the two other themes we've talked about, that the less we've been shaped by literacy, and the more oral we remain, the more intuitively we can navigate our lives? We've learned how to put our past behind us, and by doing so, we've learned to be discontent with ourselves. We've learned to substitute the idea of success through comparison to ourselves or among ourselves for that of faithfulness. Finally, we've learned to reject satisfying friendships for the emptiness of "followers" to our own emotional harm. Once again, our heads tell us one thing, but our hearts tell us another.

The fact remains that we are born, and spend the early years of our lives, as oral beings. We learn literacy over a long and arduous process of education. It takes years to develop the habits of thought that give rise to modern Western individuality and objectivity, and for many of us, that never really happens completely. Most of the world around us remains in orality, and throughout history, few cultures have attained the kind of literacy that Americans think is the norm. Remember that of the roughly 10,000 languages in the world today, fewer than 300 have their own literature. The rest have survived and flourished without reducing their history to the page only. Their identity lies in the richness of orality, and they've done quite well over the last several millennia.

And even the kind of literacy we take for granted in America is less than one hundred years old. To put it bluntly, the levels of literacy we enjoy are an outlier in the history of humanity, not the norm. Primary literacy is a blip in the history of humanity, and the end result of scientific thinking is less than positive. Our trains may run on time, and our watches measure our blood oxygen and caloric consumption in real time, but we've managed to bring ourselves to the brink of extinction in only a few centuries.

Even if we do become highly literate (and I don't just mean able to read and write; I mean that our thought processes are so shaped by the contours of the world of print that we are hard-pressed to imagine that any oral story could be true or useful), we still retain much of our early orality. It's as if we have the veneer of literacy over the core of orality, and we still yearn for the comfort of our early days before we left the garden. No matter how highly educated an audience, we still all stop and listen when the speaker says "once upon a time..." or "in a galaxy far, far away..."

One of the most interesting things about the story of Creation found in Genesis is that no one in the Bible ever quotes it or refers to it. Paul mentions it only to illustrate that nature itself teaches us the existence of God. It's only we moderns who have hung our faith on whether an origin story can be proven to the satisfaction of modern criteria. That's one of the reasons that I'm not concerned about whether the story is literally true. Asking that is like asking if the inventors of popcorn couldn't have figured out how to design it so that it doesn't burn in the microwave. The standard of "literally true" asks if there are independent written accounts, preferably hostile, that confirm the other written account. In an oral age, this is an absurd question.

In practical terms, we can ask the question, "How would it change your life if it isn't something that can be proven by modern science? Does it really matter if it's not true, as long as its truthful?" That's the standard of an oral story—not the written truth of orality, but the truthfulness of telling us what we need to know to live our lives. But there's something fascinating to be found in the story, and it's only a speculation on my part. All of the origin stories to be found across religious traditions are oral accounts, transcribed in modern terms. They all share a fall from perfection to brokenness, and they all describe the need for restoration.

All of Creation was spoken into existence, and Adam and Eve walked with the voice of God in the cool of the garden. Their temptation was to know the difference between good and evil, and to be like God Himself, and when they made that choice, they lost fellowship with God's voice as sound. They lost their connection to the creative force of their world. In their loneliness, they felt alone, naked, uncovered, and ashamed, and they hid themselves from God's voice.

When the Lord speaks to them, He asks, "Who told you that you were naked?" And it's telling that the records and accounts of sociologists who first encounter oral peoples show that the adoption of literacy coincides with the loss of identity in the oral culture. In other words, it's common for those who make the shift from orality to literacy to feel naked and ashamed of their past. They've lost the stories that give them identity, and the loss is grieved. But take heart. It's also necessary for Adam and Eve to leave and return as friends by their own choice. Much as the prodigal had to return in shame to realize that his father's offer of friendship really did cover his foolishness, Adam and Eve couldn't be raised to the status of friends unless they were separated from their Creator.

Adam and Eve have chosen to turn their back on the pure presence of God through His voice, and instead to use language to examine and know the difference between good and evil. Instead of simply being in God's presence, they have become judges of God's works. It's fascinating that historians trace the emergence of writing back to around 800–1000 BCE, the same time frame that's assigned to the writing down of the Creation story. Even if it's not literally true, Adam and Eve's story reverberates with the same anguish and remorse that oral cultures experience when they encounter literacy.

It's not a coincidence that the Word later became flesh and dwelled among us, and finally fulfilled God's purpose by sacrificing Himself, so that we might be reunited with the Father's voice. And it's also no coincidence that Paul, who of all the apostles most frequently declares the power of the spoken gospel, also tells us so much about how our own voice and our own testimony of transformation figure into our status as friends of God. Once written, the word becomes a simulacrum of what is spoken—the tracks of an event, but not the event itself.

So time becomes a line, and our past must be rejected, leaving us dissatisfied and cut off from our own story. Faithfulness becomes success: the substitution of judgment and comparison instead of the joy of knowing that He's pleased with us. Friendships become poker games, where every card that is played carries the risk that the game will end with our rejection. Or have they?

For each of these notions, we carry on with two sets of beliefs. When asked to describe success, most people really try to describe faithfulness. What does it profit us if we gain the whole world but lose our soul? When we are asked to describe how we relate to our past, most of us try to split the difference between hating our past and embracing our own story. And when asked to think about friendship, most of us try to explain it in terms of the traditional understanding while still trying to use the vocabulary of the modern paradigm. In all of these, our heads tell us one thing while our hearts tell us another.

And why not? The Word of God that we share each time we get together, and the Bread of Life we feast upon alone or in community, is spoken, not written. The Creation is spoken, not written. The Body of Christ in the earth is spoken, not written. And heaven is spoken, not written. Even though our text is written, we still must hear the voice of God in our hearts as the writing is infused with life by His Spirit. All of us speak our testimony, while a handful write about their experience. And it's in the experience of what our hearts tell all of us that we can hear the echoes of eternity.

For Further Reading

I have tried not to clutter up the reading experience by footnotes, which slow down the reading process and often introduce distractions. There is a volume of good scholarship about most of the themes I've pursued, and the following lists some of the most important. For those who wish to read further or to learn more about some of these issues, these are good starting points while being accessible to the busy pastor or leader.

Literary critics did much of the early work in exploring the differences between literacy and orality. A great starting point is *Orality and Literacy* by Walter Ong, published in 1982. Ong wrote several books exploring the implications of an oral world in the reception of Scripture. *The Presence of the Word: Some Prolegomena for Cultural and Religious History* (1967) is considered a pioneering work in several fields, including the fields of cultural studies and media ecology. His work differs from Marshall McLuhan's, in that the latter was more interested in the influence of television and advertising while Ong was more interested in the historical development of the shaping influence of literacy.

Richard Nisbett covered many of the same questions in *The Geography of Western Thought: How Asians and Westerners Think Differently* in 2003. Nisbett surveys the many studies in psychology that measure and document the differences between cultural habits of thought. The main difference between Nisbett's approach and Ong's is that Nisbett is interested in contemporary thinkers rather than historical texts. Nisbett acknowledges that literary critics have nibbled around the edges, but of course discovered nothing until psychologists came along and devised ways to measure the differences through controlled studies. Ironically, this is exactly what would come of literacy, which tends to reject the past unless it can be proven by science in the past. Nisbett suggests that the difference may lie in geography, but he still describes differences in great detail between cultures that have committed to literacy as the only way to be in the world and those who have not.

For those who want something a little more hard-headed, there is *The Oral and the Written Gospel: The Hermeneutics of Speaking and Writing in the Synoptic Tradition of Mark, Paul, and Q* by Werner H. Kelber. This work, published in 1983, goes into incredible depth regarding the differences in the ways that the Gospel writers created their works, and the differing levels of the influence of literacy on each of the writers. Fishermen compose differently than rhetoricians like Paul and other early church leaders, and Kelber is keenly interested in the influence of literacy on the development of early church theology. Kelber goes so far as to argue that the dispute between Paul and Mark was over whether writing the gospel message reduced its status as truth. Paul maintains the primacy of proclaiming the gospel, while Mark produced an account of Jesus' ministry that has many of the indicators of early novelistic style.

A more recent work by Richard Horsley and Jonathan Draper is *Whoever Hears You Hears Me: Prophets, Performance, and Tradition in Q.* The authors explore many of the same themes as Ong and Kelber applied to the preservation and use of Q. Their exploration of the interplay between orality and literacy in composition of a purely oral book of Jesus' sayings is superb.

The development of the modern self has been studied and chronicled by many scholars from many disciplines. I've drawn from Carl G.

Vaught's book *The Quest for Wholeness*. Vaught traces the development of the early through the modern self by using Abraham's relationship with YAHWEH in the Old Testament, through the middle period of national self-identity (Paul's audience), to the emergence of the modern self in nineteenth-century literature (*Moby Dick*, published in 1851.) Melville's book is a retelling of Jonah's story, and is a useful comparison to the self as expressed by both the biblical and the modern versions. The modern self is further changed from desperately isolated and fragmented (Freud and subsequent thinkers) to become the site of competing discourses of power and oppression. Vaught's *Two Meditations on Love* are the source of several insights into the depths of friendship between Jesus and Peter, as well as a succinct articulation of the relationships between agape and phileo in the Greek notions of love.

Orlando Patterson's *Freedom in the Making of Western Culture* is an invaluable resource in understanding how the idea of freedom contributed to the emergence of the modern self. Patterson traces the growth of the idea of freedom from the fifth-century BCE in Greek thought, through the changes brought by imperial Rome in Jesus' day. The relationship of freedom to slavery and oppression is critical in understanding key moments in the Bible, from Abraham's rejection of his identity (a form of suicide) to the prodigal's terrifying isolation, to Jesus' parables and the apostolic writings.

Another insightful area of study can be entered by reading *The Fall of Public Man* by Richard Sennett. This book traces how the individual's obligations to the community have changed over time. Sennet traces how the goal of Hellenistic culture was to produce a virtuous public actor, to the emergence of the modern private self and personal gratification. Sennett traces the shift of the notion of citizenship from participation to isolation, to the detriment of the public good. He is influential in raising the question of public vs. private, and how our understanding of the notion of "public" has changed from a sense of civic duty to the opposite of "private."

Sennett argues that modern thinkers regard "public" as the roads, bridges, and shared spaces that allow us to move as quickly as possible from private space to private space. The proliferation of security cameras and cell phones has further eroded privacy, such that many moderns feel that privacy no longer exists outside of not tweeting.

Friendship has gotten attention in the last few decades, perhaps as the internet and Facebook have adopted the term to mean something entirely different than it did prior to the rise of the connected self and the fragmented community. Ancient thinkers commented often about friendship, as it was a crucial part of civic life. Aristotle wrote extensively about friendship in the *Nichomachean Ethics,* which was a series of letters written by an older teacher to a young student. Aristotle's works were the backbone of instruction in and around Paul's time, and Paul's letters to Roman university towns often seem to be engaging some of Aristotle's thinking. Cicero wrote a treatise *On Friendship* around 44 BCE, and much of the thinking remained the same. More modern treatments of friendship are *Friendship in the Classical World* by David Konstan, and *Friendship in the Hebrew Bible* by Saul Olyan.

The influence of rhetoric on early church writers has also received much attention. Anyone who was educated in the first century was trained in rhetoric, the center piece of the Trivium. Aristotle defined rhetoric as "the faculty of observing in any given case what are the available means of persuasion."* This consisted of discovering what moves hearers, and why, and relates it to any topic. It placed the emphasis almost entirely on audience reception rather than message generation, on what hearers would judge credible rather than novel ideas. I've used a modern restatement of Aristotle's theory published by Lloyd Bitzer, *The Rhetorical Situation.*

Interesting sources that develop in-depth looks at the interplay of ancient rhetoric and early church theology are *The Rhetorical Origins of*

---

* The Rhetoric and Poetics of Aristotle, translated by Rhys Roberts, New York. The Modern Library 1954, 24.

the Christian Faith by Thomas Kinneavey, *Faithful Persuasion: In Aid of a Rhetoric of Christian Theology* by David Cunningham, and *New Testament Interpretation Through Rhetorical Criticism* by George Kennedy. For an outstanding look at how the study of Greek rhetoric shaped the thinking of Augustine and succeeding theologians, there's *Temporality, Eternity, and Wisdom: The Rhetoric of Augustine's Confessions* by Calvin Troup. Finally, for an insightful application of the differences between prose and poetry (proclamation) in preaching, there's *Finally Comes the Poet* by Walter Brueggeman.

Acknowledgments

I'm blessed to have had a career that encompassed four basic elements: read a lot, think a lot, talk a lot, and write a lot. And along the way there have been friends who have been invaluable in sharpening my thinking about some of the ideas I like to explore. To the many friends who have had their kidneys challenged in coffee shops and classrooms through the years and across the country, many thanks.

In particular, I want to thank my early readers Anton Goyak, Sam and Kris Wood, Norm Leatherwood, Jim and Sally Godlewski. Your comments, questions, and challenges have been invaluable in helping me determine if this is worth seeing the light of day, or merely a long honk by an old guy with a burr under his saddle.

To the many colleagues and friends who have encouraged me by listening: Dick McDonald, Bill Eck, Brian Wood, Steve Schmick, Dave Johnson, Carl Kramer, Alan Cleveland, Greg Macheel, Kurt Klemm, thank you.

To my family, who have endured incessant lectures without complaint, Ryan and Sarah, thank you. I'm so proud of you both!

To Theresa, who has been my partner and love of my life for the last forty-five years, thank you!

Finally, to editors Christy Lemire at Avodah Literary Services, Geoff Stone at Illumify Media, and the entire Illumify team, thank you for invaluable help in letting this project speak.

About the Author

Greg Books earned a PhD in communication from the Pennsylvania State University in 1996. In addition to two decades of university teaching and administration, he's served as a senior executive in non-profit and for-profit organizations. Greg has served as a founding pastor, teaching pastor, and national program coordinator of campus ministry. He especially enjoys teaching men's retreats around the theme of stronger friendships.

Greg has consulted in private industry as a speech writer, executive trainer, organizational transition planner, and crisis communication leader. Greg has been a frequent speaker and writer in areas as diverse as patent law and dental equipment design, applied ergonomics, and entrepreneurial startups. His research interests in technology and virtual communities have resulted in many conference papers and presentations. In his spare time, Greg enjoys restoring British sports cars and vintage racing.

Contact: Gregory Books, 735 East Scott Street, Omro WI 54963, 920-500-0808, Greg@drgregbooks.com

www.ingramcontent.com/pod-product-compliance
Lightning Source LLC
Chambersburg PA
CBHW021718120626
46545CB00004B/1615